Exam Ref DP-100 Designing and Implementing a Data Science Solution on Azure

Dayne Sorvisto

Exam Ref DP-100 Designing and Implementing a Data Science Solution on Azure

Published with the authorization of Microsoft Corporation by:
Pearson Education, Inc.

ISBN-13: 978-0-13-535060-7
ISBN-10: 0-13-535060-3

Library of Congress Control Number: 2024946348

1 2024

TRADEMARKS

Microsoft and the trademarks listed at http://www.microsoft.com on the "Trademarks" webpage are trademarks of the Microsoft group of companies. All other marks are property of their respective owners.

WARNING AND DISCLAIMER

Every effort has been made to make this book as complete and as accurate as possible, but no warranty or fitness is implied. The information provided is on an "as is" basis. The author, the publisher, and Microsoft Corporation shall have neither liability nor responsibility to any person or entity with respect to any loss or damages arising from the information contained in this book or from the use of the programs accompanying it.

SPECIAL SALES

For information about buying this title in bulk quantities, or for special sales opportunities (which may include electronic versions; custom cover designs; and content particular to your business, training goals, marketing focus, or branding interests), please contact our corporate sales department at corpsales@pearsoned.com or (800) 382-3419.

For government sales inquiries, please contact governmentsales@pearsoned.com.

For questions about sales outside the U.S., please contact intlcs@pearson.com.

CREDITS

EDITOR-IN-CHIEF
Brett Bartow

EXECUTIVE EDITOR
Loretta Yates

ASSOCIATE EDITOR
Shourav Bose

DEVELOPMENT EDITOR
Songlin Qiu

MANAGING EDITOR
Sandra Schroeder

SENIOR PROJECT EDITOR
Tracey Croom

TECHNICAL EDITOR
Francesco Esposito

COPY EDITOR
Dan Foster

INDEXER
Timothy Wright

PROOFREADER
Barbara Mack

EDITORIAL ASSISTANT
Cindy Teeters

COVER DESIGNER
Twist Creative, Seattle

COMPOSITOR AND GRAPHICS
codeMantra

Contents at a glance

Contents

Acknowledgments

I'd like to thank my mom Allison and wife Kirsten for their insights, love, and support during the development of this book. I would also like to acknowledge my late grandfather Bruce for his advice and motivation and my dog Lucy for all the hours she kept me company while writing.

About the Author

DAYNE SORVISTO is a seasoned data engineer and technical author (*MLOps Lifecycle Toolkit*). Dayne has held senior technical positions including Staff Data Engineer, Software Developer, and Senior Machine Learning Engineer, and has a Master's degree in Pure Mathematics. You can connect with Dayne on LinkedIn at *linkedin.com/in/daynesorvisto* or visit his website *wyattsolutions.co* to learn more.

Introduction

This book is intended to cover all the skills measured in the exam DP-100 Designing and Implementing a Data Science Solution on Azure. You'll find in each chapter a combination of step-by-step instructional content as well as accompanying high-level theoretical material. The aim is to show you the buttons you need to click in order to carry out the tasks required as well as covering key concepts that you need to understand when designing a data science solution. Ultimately, we cover not only the how but also the why.

This book is written for IT professionals who intend to take the DP-100 exam as well as data engineers, data scientists, and other data professionals who want to learn to design and implement a data science solution in Azure. In addition to the exam material, the book is meant to enrich your knowledge of Azure Machine Learning by using it to implement machine learning operations in Azure and to design end-to-end data science solutions.

This book covers every major topic area found on the exam, but it does not cover every exam question. Only the Microsoft exam team has access to the exam questions, and Microsoft regularly adds new questions to the exam, making it impossible to cover specific questions. You should consider this book a supplement to your relevant real-world experience and other study materials. If you encounter a topic in this book that you do not feel completely comfortable with, use the "Need more review?" links you'll find in the text to find more information and take the time to research and study the topic.

Organization of this book

This book is organized by the "Skills measured" list published for the exam. The "Skills measured" list is available for each exam on the Microsoft Learn website: *microsoft.com/learn*. Each chapter in this book corresponds to a major topic area in the list, and the technical tasks in each topic area determine a chapter's organization. If an exam covers six major topic areas, for example, the book will contain six chapters.

Preparing for the exam

Microsoft certification exams are a great way to build your résumé and let the world know about your level of expertise. Certification exams validate your on-the-job experience and product knowledge. Although there is no substitute for on-the-job experience, preparation through study and hands-on practice can help you prepare for the exam. This book is *not* designed to teach you new skills.

We recommend that you augment your exam preparation plan by using a combination of available study materials and courses. For example, you might use the *Exam Ref* and another study guide for your at-home preparation and take a Microsoft Official Curriculum course for the classroom experience. Choose the combination that you think works best for you. Learn more about available classroom training, online courses, and live events at *microsoft.com/learn*.

Note that this *Exam Ref* is based on publicly available information about the exam and the author's experience. To safeguard the integrity of the exam, authors do not have access to the live exam.

Microsoft certifications

Microsoft certifications distinguish you by proving your command of a broad set of skills and experience with current Microsoft products and technologies. The exams and corresponding certifications are developed to validate your mastery of critical competencies as you design and develop, or implement and support, solutions with Microsoft products and technologies both onpremises and in the cloud. Certification brings a variety of benefits to the individual and to employers and organizations.

> *MORE INFO* **ALL MICROSOFT CERTIFICATIONS**
>
> For information about Microsoft certifications, including a full list of available certifications, go to *microsoft.com/learn*.

Access the Exam Updates chapter and online references

The final chapter of this book, "Exam DP-100: Designing and Implementing a Data Science Solution on Azure—updates" will be used to provide information about new content per new exam topics, content that has been removed from the exam objectives, and revised mapping of exam objectives to chapter content. The chapter will be made available from the link below as exam updates are released.

Throughout this book are addresses to webpages that the author has recommended you visit for more information. Some of these links can be very long and painstaking to type, so we've shortened them for you to make them easier to visit. We've also compiled them into a single list that readers of the print edition can refer to while they read.

The URLs are organized by chapter and heading. Every time you come across a URL in the book, find the hyperlink in the list to go directly to the webpage.

Download the Exam Updates chapter and the URL list at
MicrosoftPressStore.com/ERDP100/downloads

Errata, updates, & book support

We've made every effort to ensure the accuracy of this book and its companion content. You can access updates to this book—in the form of a list of submitted errata and their related corrections—at:

MicrosoftPressStore.com/ERDP100/errata

If you discover an error that is not already listed, please submit it to us at the same page.

For additional book support and information, please visit *MicrosoftPressStore.com/Support*.

Please note that product support for Microsoft software and hardware is not offered through the previous addresses. For help with Microsoft software or hardware, go to *support.microsoft.com*.

Stay in touch

Let's keep the conversation going! We're on X / Twitter: *twitter.com/MicrosoftPress*.

## CHAPTER 1

Design and prepare a machine learning solution

Managing machine learning models in a production environment requires careful consideration. Data science research and development code can be messy, written in notebooks or with data managed in spreadsheets. Data scientists who specialize in machine learning operations (MLOps) are responsible for taking research and development code and deploying it to production.

We need to carefully balance the needs of the business with the performance of the models and translate the requirements into a solution that covers compute and storage as well as handling of both code and data. The latter, handling of data sources, represents a significant enough fork from other kinds of software engineering that it implores its own set of best practices. For example, we need best practices around data and model management to ensure that our solution can handle real-world scenarios such as data drift, model drift, different versions of data, and changing schemas.

In many data science projects, some of the challenge exists in managing many aspects of the machine learning lifecycle. A major shift in how we view this lifecycle comes with the advent of large language models (LLM)s, increased regulatory requirements on model fairness, and the need to deal with massive volumes of data.

In this chapter, we navigate the initial phase of the machine learning lifecycle in Azure, focusing on design, management, and optimization. We begin with a design-first approach where we lay the foundation for designing and preparing a machine learning solution, covering compute specifications, deployment requirements, and development approaches that should provide you with a holistic overview of the entire lifecycle.

Next, we dive into the operational aspects of creating and managing a workspace. This includes using developer tools for workspace interactions and setting up Git integration for source control. We will also explore selecting Azure storage resources, registering and maintaining datastores, and creating and managing data assets.

Finally, we will round out the chapter by guiding you through creating compute targets, selecting data science environments for different use cases, configuring Apache Spark tools, and monitoring resources.

By the end of this chapter, you will have a holistic understanding of the key components involved in designing and preparing a machine learning solution in Azure, setting the stage for the subsequent phases of the machine learning lifecycle.

Skills covered in this chapter:

- Skill 1.1: Design a machine learning solution
- Skill 1.2: Manage an Azure Machine Learning workspace
- Skill 1.3: Manage data in an Azure Machine Learning workspace
- Skill 1.4: Manage compute for experiments in Azure Machine Learning

Skill 1.1: Design a machine learning solution

The data science lifecycle can be separated into phases like training and inference but can include nuanced steps like fine-tuning or reinforcement learning steps. We can begin to ask how we can evaluate and determine the appropriate computer specifications for specific phases. In this section, we will look at training workloads only.

> **This skill covers how to:**
> - Determine the appropriate compute specifications for a training workload
> - Describe model deployment requirements
> - Select which development approach to use to build or train a model

Determine the appropriate compute specifications for a training workload

As you expand your training with larger datasets or engage in distributed training, utilize Azure Machine Learning compute to establish a cluster with single or multiple nodes that automatically scale whenever you submit a job. Additionally, you have the option to connect your own compute resource, although the level of support may differ across various scenarios.

One interesting property of compute targets in Azure Machine Learning is that they can be reused across training jobs, and you only have to attach the compute target to the workspace once to use it again in other jobs. Your data science development workflow might look like the following:

1. Begin by working with a small dataset in your local environment, such as a local computer or a cloud-based virtual machine (VM).

2. As you progress, scale up to larger datasets or engage in distributed training by utilizing suitable training compute targets.

Given that you have faced the above, how can you determine the appropriate compute specifications for a training workload in Azure Machine Learning? It helps to consider the following factors:

- **Model complexity** More complex models, such as deep learning models (for example, an NLP—natural language processing—model you create in PyTorch), may require higher compute power for tensor operations and memory. Even shallow models like random forests may be memory intensive. A machine learning model can be an implementation of a learning algorithm with a given architecture. It is therefore important to understand the underlying architecture and algorithm behind the model.

- **Data size** Large datasets may require more memory and storage. If you batch your dataset, for example, the batch should fit in memory, so your compute target must have enough memory for a batch.

- **Training duration** Long training times may benefit from more powerful compute resources to reduce overall training time and determine the choice between VMs configured to use CPUs/GPUs for an Azure ML compute instance and distributed training scenario.

Azure Machine Learning provides various compute options, including Azure ML compute instances for development and testing, and Azure ML compute clusters for distributed training. There are other compute targets in preview such as Apache Spark pools. Table 1-1 summarizes some of the options (for training targets only). The difference between training and inference is that inference requires a trained model to make a prediction.

TABLE 1-1 Compute environments available in Azure Machine Learning

Compute Environment	Training Targets	Automated ML	ML Pipelines	Azure ML Designer
Local computer	Yes			
Azure ML compute cluster	Yes	Yes	Yes	Yes
Azure ML serverless compute	Yes	Yes	Yes	Yes
Azure ML compute instance	Yes (SDK)	Yes	Yes	Yes
Azure ML Kubernetes		Yes	Yes	
Remote VM	Yes	Yes		
Apache Spark pools (preview)	Yes (SDK local)	Yes		
Azure Databricks	Yes (SDK local)	Yes		

Understanding compute targets

If you study Table 1-1, you can list all the compute targets available. You'll notice that Azure ML compute instances (single VMs) are a managed cloud-based workstation for data scientists. Each of these instances has a single owner, and you can share files between compute instances.

IT administrators can use onboard management features for managing these instances. Therefore, Azure ML compute instances have a dual purpose, serving as both compute targets and as fully configurable, managed development environments for data science. Azure Machine Learning introduces the concept of a *compute target*. Broadly speaking, we can categorize compute targets into the following types:

- Azure ML compute includes both instances and clusters. These are for single or multi-node clusters that autoscale for each job submission. This is suitable for scaling up training on larger datasets (remember, dataset size was a factor in choosing a compute or performing distributed training).

- Remote VM: Attach a remote VM to your workspace for reuse in multiple jobs. For machine learning pipelines, utilize the appropriate pipeline step for each compute target. There are several VM sizes available, and you can select VMs in terms of memory and compute. (We'll cover this in-depth later in this section.)

- Serverless, Spark Pools (see Figure 1-1), and Databricks: Azure Databricks can be used as a training resource for local runs and machine learning pipelines but not as a remote target for other training scenarios. There are also serverless options and Spark Pools, which we will cover in-depth later.

The third category highlights another way to think about compute in Azure Machine Learning in terms of managed and unmanaged compute targets.

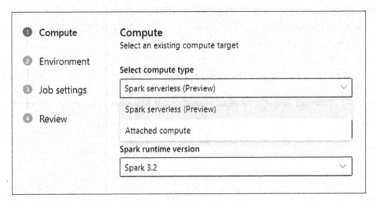

FIGURE 1-1 Serverless Spark compute type

Managed compute targets

Azure Machine Learning manages these compute resources, optimized for machine learning workloads. Managed compute includes compute clusters, compute instances, and serverless compute.

One point of interest is serverless compute targets. Azure Machine Learning has a serverless compute option that allows you to train models without the need for managing compute resources (hence why we say "managed compute"). This fully managed, on-demand compute scales and manages itself, freeing you up to focus on building machine learning models.

You can specify the resources needed for each job, and Azure Machine Learning takes care of the rest, including network isolation. This simplifies the process but also helps reduce costs by optimizing resources. Additionally, you have control over the cores quota (the maximum number of cores that can be allocated to your resources within a region or subscription) at both the subscription and workspace levels, and you can apply Azure policies. This is important for machine learning architects to understand because if you have a tenant with multiple subscriptions, you can have different Azure policies and quotas for each.

Serverless compute supports a variety of tasks, including fine-tuning models like *LLAMA 2*, running jobs from Azure Machine Learning Studio, SDK, and CLI, building environment images, and responsible AI dashboard scenarios. It consumes the same quota as Azure Machine Learning compute and offers the choice between standard (dedicated) and spot (low priority) VMs, with both managed and user identity support. The billing model remains the same as for Azure Machine Learning compute.

> **NEED MORE REVIEW? SENSITIVE COMPUTE TARGETS**
>
> You can read more about serverless compute and cost-saving options like using spot VMs here: *https://learn.microsoft.com/en-us/azure/machine-learning/how-to-use-serverless-compute*

Azure Machine Learning also supports unmanaged compute types such as remote virtual machines, Azure Databricks, and Kubernetes. These require additional maintenance steps or performance tuning for machine learning workloads.

Assessing model complexity and data size

You should evaluate the complexity of your machine learning model and the size of your dataset to determine the computational power and memory required. Consider factors such as the type of algorithms, the number of features, and the volume of data to be processed.

In the context of assessing model complexity and data size for determining the appropriate compute specifications for a training workload in Azure Machine Learning, the article "Prevent overfitting and imbalanced data with Automated ML" (*https://learn.microsoft.com/en-us/azure/machine-learning/concept-manage-ml-pitfalls*) provides relevant insights.

Introducing model complexity

The complexity of your machine learning model, including the type of algorithms used, can impact the likelihood of overfitting. Complex models with many parameters, such as deep learning networks, are more prone to overfitting, especially when trained on small datasets.

Automated ML in Azure Machine Learning provides mechanisms like regularization and model complexity limitations to prevent overfitting, which is crucial for maintaining a balance between model complexity and generalization ability.

So how does this translate into increased compute requirements for your workload? The size of your dataset and the balance between different classes play a significant role in model performance. For example, imbalanced datasets, where one class significantly outnumbers others, can lead to models that are biased toward the majority class. One solution is to use Auto ML, which has built-in features to handle imbalanced data, such as generating a weight column to adjust the importance of different classes. Another solution might be to upsample or use a more robust algorithm like random forests that can handle the imbalance. However, as with many solutions there are trade-offs, and a particularly important trade-off is computational power and memory required, as balancing the data might necessitate additional computational resources.

The choice of algorithm in Automated ML can also influence the computational requirements. Algorithms that are more robust to imbalanced data or that inherently incorporate regularization might reduce the need for extensive computational resources. Table 1-2 shows a comparison of different algorithms for handling imbalanced datasets, including Random Over-Sampling, Random Under-Sampling, SMOTE, ADASYN, Cost-Sensitive Learning, and Ensemble Methods. The table displays two columns for each algorithm, representing their relative memory intensity and compute intensity, with labels ranging from Low to High.

TABLE 1-2 Table of memory and compute requirements for various algorithms

Algorithm	Description	Memory Intensity	Compute Intensity
Random Over-Sampling	Duplicates instances from the minority class to balance the dataset	Low	Low
Random Under-Sampling	Removes instances from the majority class to balance the dataset	Low	Low
SMOTE (Synthetic Minority Over-Sampling Technique)	Generates synthetic instances for the minority class	Medium	High
ADASYN (Adaptive Synthetic Sampling)	Similar to SMOTE but generates synthetic samples in a way that shifts the decision boundary	Medium	High
Cost-Sensitive Learning	Assigns different costs to different classes, penalizing the misclassification of minority classes more	Low	Medium
Ensemble Methods (e.g., Balanced Random Forest, RUSBoost)	Combines multiple models to improve performance on imbalanced datasets	High	High

Limitations of model complexity in Azure Machine Learning

In Azure Machine Learning's Automated ML, model complexity limitations are enforced to prevent overfitting. This is particularly relevant for decision tree or forest algorithms, where constraints are applied to limit the maximum depth of individual trees as well as the total number of trees used in forest or ensemble methods. These limitations help ensure that the models remain generalizable and avoid fitting too closely to the training data.

> **NEED MORE REVIEW?** **REFERENCE MATERIALS FOR TRAINING PITFALLS**
>
> You can read more about ML pitfalls, including how to prevent overfitting and underfitting in your solution, by visiting the official documentation here: *https://learn.microsoft.com/en-us/azure/machine-learning/concept-manage-ml-pitfalls?view=azureml-api-2*

Selecting virtual machine (VM) sizes

In Azure Machine Learning, when selecting a node size for a managed compute resource, you can choose from a variety of VM sizes that Azure offers for both Linux and Windows, catering to different workloads. However, there are some exceptions and limitations to keep in mind. Not all VM series are supported in Azure Machine Learning, and certain series, such as GPUs and other special SKUs, may not be immediately visible in your list of available VMs. To use these, you'll need to request a quota change. For more details on supported series and requesting quotas, refer to the documentation on VM types and sizes and quota requests.

You can explore the available VM sizes in Azure Machine Learning, ranging from general-purpose to high-performance compute options. Selecting a compute target will ultimately translate into matching the VM size to your workload requirements, considering factors such as CPU, GPU, memory, and storage needs based on workload factors like model complexity and dataset size.

It is sometimes necessary to perform a combination of performance testing to create estimates for memory and storage needs, but you should also do back-of-the-envelope calculations to estimate the workload requirements into the future—for example, based on the numbers of users of the model and the number of data scientists on your team. If you have a streaming source that produces 2 GB per day, then you will want to ensure that you have enough storage to meet future storage needs, so you should factor this in when choosing a VM for your commute instance or cluster. Here's a summary of key points to consider for different VMs: Table 1-3 shows types of virtual machines (VMs) and their use cases.

TABLE 1-3 Virtual machine (VM) types and their use cases

VM Type	CPU-to-Memory Ratio	Ideal Use Cases
General Purpose VMs	Balanced	Testing and development, small to medium databases
Compute Optimized VMs	High	Medium traffic web servers, network appliances, batch processes
Memory Optimized VMs	High memory-to-CPU	Relational database servers, medium to large caches, in-memory analytics

VM Type	CPU-to-Memory Ratio	Ideal Use Cases
Storage Optimized VMs	High disk throughput	Big Data, SQL, NoSQL databases, data warehousing
GPU VMs	Specialized	Model training with deep learning, custom models, or matrix operations
High Performance Compute VMs	Fastest CPU	Optional high-throughput network interfaces (RDMA)

When assessing model complexity and data size, consider the type of VM that best fits your workload. For example, use GPU VMs for deep learning model training or memory-optimized VMs for large-scale batch data processing. You can manage costs effectively by using Azure Cost Management to set budgets, configure alerts, and optimize your Azure costs.

> **IMPORTANT   SELECTING VIRTUAL MACHINE SIZES FOR WORKLOADS**
>
> When selecting a virtual machine (VM) size for your Azure Machine Learning workload, consider the specific requirements of your machine learning model and dataset. For instance, if your model involves deep learning, a GPU VM like the NC series may be more suitable due to its specialized hardware for model training.
>
> On the other hand, if your workload involves large datasets or in-memory analytics, a memory-optimized VM such as the Esv3 or Ev3 series might be a better fit. Always balance performance needs with cost considerations and remember that you can scale up or down as your requirements change.

> **NEED MORE REVIEW?   GPU OPTIMIZED VIRTUAL MACHINES**
>
> You can read more about using GPU optimized VMs via the following link to official Microsoft documentation on sizes for GPU-enabled VMs: *https://learn.microsoft.com/en-us/azure/virtual-machines/sizes-gpu*.

Again, remember that you can always scale up or scale down resources when requirements change. The next section covers what happens when you have an unpredictable workload, and you are unable to measure exact memory and compute requirements for the workload because they depend on external factors.

Scaling compute resources

What happens if you have an unpredictable workload? For example, consider the scenario where you need to have more data available to train based on demand. The concept of *autoscaling* is extremely important in these real-world scenarios because it can be used in a cloud computing environment to dynamically scale your workloads based on requirements.

Configure training clusters for autoscaling

You can use Azure ML compute clusters, AmlCompute, that scale dynamically based on workload requirements. Set the minimum nodes to 0 to avoid charges when no jobs are running.

In Azure Machine Learning, This means that the cluster can scale up to accommodate increased demand for computational resources and scale down when the demand decreases, helping to manage costs and ensure efficient resource utilization. Let's look at how autoscaling works in Azure Machine Learning.

> **NOTE   MINIMUM NODE SETTINGS**
>
> When creating or updating an AmlCompute cluster, you can configure autoscaling settings, including the minimum and maximum number of nodes. The minimum nodes setting determines the number of nodes that are always available (which can be zero), while the maximum nodes setting caps the number of nodes that can be provisioned.

- **Scaling Up**   When a new job is submitted to the cluster and there are not enough available nodes to run the job, the cluster automatically scales up by provisioning additional nodes, up to the maximum number specified. This ensures that jobs can start without waiting for manual intervention.

- **Scaling Down**   After a job is completed, if there are idle nodes in the cluster, the autoscaling feature starts deallocating these nodes based on the idle time settings (see Figure 1-2). If the number of nodes falls below the minimum specified, the cluster stops deallocating nodes to maintain the minimum level of availability.

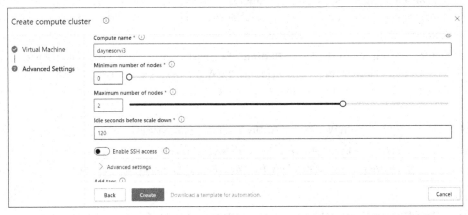

FIGURE 1-2 User interface for creating a compute cluster in Azure Machine Learning and scaling options

Cost management

Autoscaling helps manage costs by reducing the number of idle nodes when they are not needed, thereby minimizing unnecessary charges. By setting the minimum nodes to 0, you can ensure that you're not charged for compute resources when no jobs are running.

How else can you manage resources and costs during training? Here are a few features available that can help you manage resources:

- **Set Quotas on Resources**   Control the amount of AmlCompute resources available in your subscription and workspaces by setting quotas by VM family and region.
- **Set Job Autotermination Policies**   Configure training runs to limit their duration or terminate them early to save costs, using parameters like max_run_duration_seconds and early termination policies for hyperparameter tuning and automated machine learning.
- **Use Low-Priority VMs**   Utilize excess unutilized capacity as Low-Priority VMs for batch workloads and recoverable tasks, which come at a reduced price compared to dedicated VMs.
- **Schedule Compute Instances**   Enable idle shutdown or set up a schedule to automatically start and stop compute instances to save costs when they are not in use.
- **Use Reserved Instances**   Purchase Azure Reserved VM Instances for one-year or three-year terms to receive discounts on compute resources.
- **Parallelize Training**   Optimize cost and performance by parallelizing the workload using parallel components in Azure Machine Learning.
- **Set Data Retention and Deletion Policies**   Manage intermediate datasets generated during pipeline execution by setting policies to archive and delete datasets to optimize storage costs.
- **Deploy Resources to the Same Region**   Reduce network latency and data transfer costs by deploying all resources, including the Azure Machine Learning workspace and dependent resources, in the same region as your data.

Describe model deployment requirements

When determining the requirements for your model deployment, consider factors such as the expected traffic, latency requirements, cost constraints, and the level of control you need over the deployment environment. Each deployment target has its own set of trade-offs, so it's essential to choose the one that aligns best with your application's needs and the characteristics of your model (see Figure 1-3).

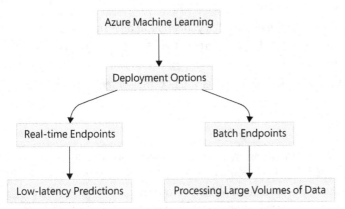

FIGURE 1-3 Model deployment options in Azure Machine Learning

Describing model deployment requirements in Azure Machine Learning involves understanding various aspects that influence how a model is deployed and managed. Here is a checklist of requirements you should consider in a real-world scenario:

- **Latency Requirements** Consider how quickly the model needs to provide predictions. Real-time applications may require low-latency responses, making managed online endpoints a suitable choice.

- **Scalability** Assess the expected traffic and workload. If you anticipate high variability in traffic or need to handle large volumes of requests, consider using Azure Kubernetes Service (AKS) for its dynamic scaling capabilities.

- **Cost Constraints** Evaluate your budget for the deployment. Azure Container Instances (ACI) can be a cost-effective option for development and testing, while batch endpoints may be more economical for processing large datasets.

- **Data Volume** Determine the size of the data that the model will process. Batch endpoints are well-suited for large datasets that do not require immediate processing.

- **Model Complexity** Consider the complexity of the model and its dependencies. AKS may provide more flexibility for deploying complex models that require custom configurations or specific dependencies.

- **Security Requirements** Ensure that the deployment target meets your application's security requirements. Managed online endpoints offer built-in security features such as authentication and TLS (SSL) termination.

- **Management Overhead** Assess the level of control and management you need over the deployment environment. Managed services like online endpoints and ACI offer a more hands-off approach, while AKS provides more control at the cost of increased management complexity.

- **Integration with Other Services** Consider how the deployment will integrate with other Azure services or external systems. Ensure that the chosen deployment target supports the necessary integrations for your application.

- **Compliance and Regulatory Requirements** If your application is subject to regulatory constraints, make sure that the deployment target complies with the relevant regulations and standards.

In the next section, we will look at deployment targets and how they differ from compute targets.

Deployment targets

We covered compute targets available for model training, and there are also deployment targets depending on requirements, including whether you have a real-time scenario or can batch the data you receive for the model to process. Table 1-4 compares Azure deployment options for machine learning models, including Managed Online Endpoints, Batch Endpoints, Azure Kubernetes Service (AKS), and Azure Container Instances (ACI). The table highlights ideal use cases and key characteristics of each option, such as scalability, management, and suitability for real-time inference or batch processing.

TABLE 1-4 Comparison of Azure deployment options for machine learning models

Deployment Option	Ideal Use Cases	Characteristics
Managed Online Endpoints	Real-time inference, low-latency responses	Fully managed, scalable, secure
Batch Endpoints	Overnight scoring, periodic retraining	Suitable for large volumes of data, no real-time need
Azure Kubernetes Service (AKS)	Custom configurations, variable workloads	Scalable, control over deployment, dynamic scaling
Azure Container Instances (ACI)	Development and testing, lightweight deployments	Cost-effective, easy setup, no infrastructure management

> **IMPORTANT: TRAINING A MODEL IN BATCH VERSUS BATCH INFERENCE**
>
> Training a model in batch does not imply that your model can be deployed in a batch inference scenario without further planning. For example, there may be additional requirements for inferences around latency. You may require that an inference be computed with a sub-second latency, and in this scenario you would need to consider online endpoints as a deployment target.

Managed online endpoints

When deploying managed online endpoints in Azure Machine Learning, it's important to account for the 20% quota allocation for upgrades. If you request a specific number of instances for deployment, ensure that you have enough quota for 1.2 times the number of instances, multiplied by the number of cores for the VM SKU you're using. For instance, for 10 instances of Standard_DS3_v2 VMs (each with four cores), you'll need a quota for 48 cores (ceil(1.2 * 10) * 4). To avoid errors, check your usage and request quota increases as needed in the Azure portal.

NEED MORE REVIEW?   **USING ONLINE ENDPOINTS**

For the exam, you can read more about deployment to online endpoints at *https:// learn.microsoft.com/en-us/azure/machine-learning/how-to-deploy-online-endpoints*

Model packaging and containerization

You might have noticed that Azure Container Instances (ACI) are a deployment target. Docker containers for deployment, including the creation of scoring scripts, environment configuration, and container image creation is a strategy when you need more control over the environment your model needs to make an inference.

EXAM TIP

Understand the role of Azure Container Registry in storing and managing container images for model deployment. The Azure Container Registry allows you to store binaries like images for each of your containers as well as associate tags with these images to simplify the management of container images.

Security and access control

An important requirement for deploying a model is security (see Figure 1-4 for a detailed breakdown). Security considerations for model deployment, including network isolation, private endpoints, and encryption of data in transit and at rest factor into choosing a deployment strategy.

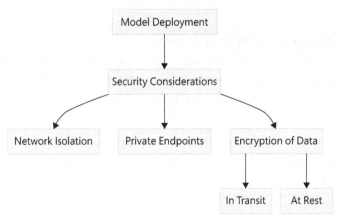

FIGURE 1-4 Model deployment security considerations

Select a development approach for building or training a model

To choose a development approach for training a model in Azure Machine Learning, consider the following options in Table 1-5 based on your project requirements.

TABLE 1-5 Development approaches to model development used to build or train a model

Development Approach	Description
Azure Machine Learning SDK for Python	A code-first solution offering various training methods, including the command() function and Automated Machine Learning
Automated Machine Learning	A low-code solution that automates algorithm selection and hyperparameter tuning, accessible for users with varying levels of expertise
Machine Learning Pipelines	A method to define a workflow with modular, reusable steps that can include training, useful for scheduling unattended processes and coordinating steps across resources
Azure Machine Learning Designer	A low-code, visual interface for training models using drag-and-drop components, suitable for building proof of concepts or for users with little coding experience
Azure CLI	A tool for scripting and automating tasks, providing commands for submitting training jobs using run configurations or pipelines

Each of these methods can utilize various compute resources, referred to as compute targets, which can be local machines or cloud resources such as Azure Machine Learning Compute or Azure HDInsight.

EXAM TIP

Understand how to configure authentication and authorization for access control to deployed endpoints, using mechanisms such as token-based authentication and role-based access control (RBAC).

NEED MORE REVIEW? **DEVELOPMENT APPROACHES DEFINED**

You can read more about different development approaches available in Azure Machine Learning and choose the one that best suits your project requirements at *https:// learn.microsoft.com/en-us/azure/machine-learning/concept-train-machine-learning-model*

In the next section, we will look at managing an Azure Machine Learning workspace and performing various tasks in the workspace so you can start development regardless of the development approach you have chosen for your project. We will also look at some best practices around organizing workspaces for projects that can help with development.

Skill 1.2: Manage an Azure Machine Learning workspace

The workspace is the top-level resource in Azure Machine Learning, so it makes sense to cover this before providing more details about attaching compute targets to experiments or working with data sources since conceptually, under the workspace, you have storage, compute targets, and models and can access experiments. In this section, we'll look at the basics of creating a workspace.

> **This skill covers how to:**
> - Create an Azure Machine Learning workspace
> - Set up Git integration for source control

Create an Azure Machine Learning workspace

You must create a workspace before you can use it. It is important to understand how to create a workspace. Workspaces can be created by using the Azure Machine Learning Studio in the Azure portal, from a VS Code extension, Azure Resource Manager/Bicep templates, Azure Machine Learning CLI or SDK, or by using REST APIs to interact with Azure Resource Manager directly. It may be simpler to view this as a step-by-step procedure for creating a workspace in the Azure portal:

1. Sign in to the Azure portal.
2. Click Create A Resource and search for "Machine Learning."
3. Select Machine Learning and click Create.
4. Fill in the required fields, such as Subscription, Resource Group, Name, and Region.
5. Review and create the workspace (see Figure 1-5).

EXAM TIP

The key pieces of information you need when creating a workspace are the subscription, resource group, workspace name, and region.

The Azure Machine Learning workspace is a foundational resource for machine learning operations in Azure. It serves as a centralized environment for collaborating with colleagues, creating machine learning artifacts, and grouping related work such as experiments, jobs, datasets, models, components, and inference endpoints. In the next section, we will look at some of the specific tasks you can perform in the workspace.

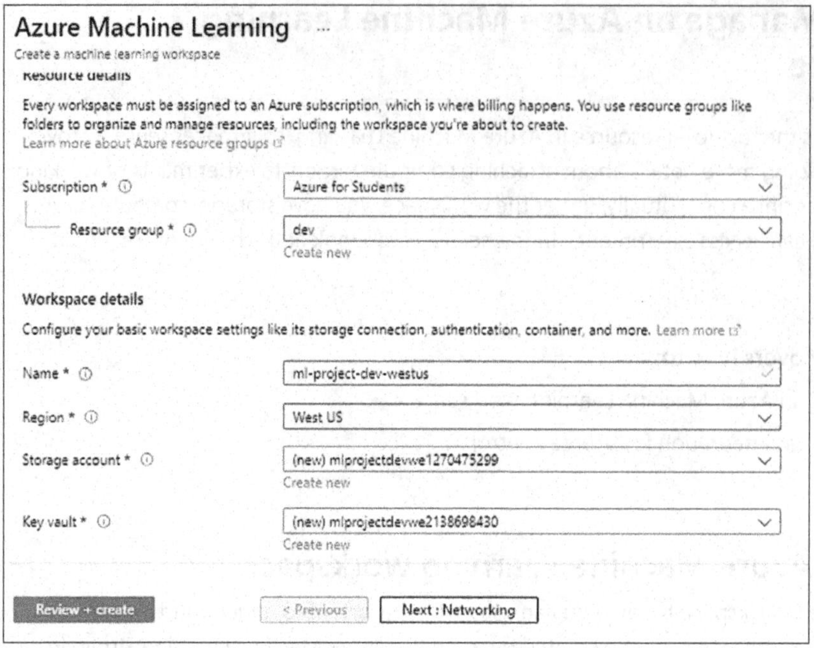

Azure Machine Learning

Create a machine learning workspace

Resource details

Every workspace must be assigned to an Azure subscription, which is where billing happens. You use resource groups like folders to organize and manage resources, including the workspace you're about to create.
Learn more about Azure resource groups ⬦

Subscription * ⓘ	Azure for Students ⌄
└ Resource group * ⓘ	dev ⌄
	Create new

Workspace details

Configure your basic workspace settings like its storage connection, authentication, container, and more. Learn more ⬦

Name * ⓘ	ml-project-dev-westus ✓
Region * ⓘ	West US ⌄
Storage account * ⓘ	(new) mlprojectdevwe1270475299 ⌄
	Create new
Key vault * ⓘ	(new) mlprojectdevwe2138698430 ⌄
	Create new

[Review + create]   [< Previous] [Next : Networking]

FIGURE 1-5 Creating an Azure Machine Learning workspace

Tasks performed within a workspace

One key task is creating jobs within a workspace. Let's look at how we can perform several tasks in a workspace through the lens of a job. We can then understand the relationship between a job, a compute target, and a workspace. We can define a job as a single task or a set of tasks that get submitted to the Azure Machine Learning resource and are scheduled for execution. An example of a job could be a training job used to train a model.

First, we know that jobs are created and managed within a workspace. This allows you to organize and track your machine learning experiments and workflows in a structured manner. Jobs use compute resources (compute targets of which we learned there are many types) that are registered and managed within the workspace. This includes resources for training models, such as Azure ML Compute clusters for distributed training. When a job is executed, Azure ML creates a *run record* within a workspace. This record includes information about the job, such as metadata, metrics, logs, and artifacts. These records are organized under experiments, which are logical groupings of runs in a workspace.

Organizing workspaces

You can create as many workspaces as you need and organize them by project. For example, you can create a workspace per project for better cost reporting and data isolation. Since workspaces also allow you to define custom user roles for permission management between different user types (for example, data scientist, machine learning engineer, admin), having separate workspaces per project with different RBAC policies can help organize your code, models, and data. For example, one useful workspace may be for R&D to allow data scientists with a data science role to work in a self-service fashion while having separate dev, test, or production workspaces.

With many workspaces you can also share Azure resources (for example, storage or compute or Azure machine learning registries for models) across workspaces to save on setup steps and costs. The workspace keeps a history of all training runs including logs, metrics, output, lineage metadata, and a snapshot of scripts. Artifacts generated during tasks in Azure Machine Learning have their metadata and data stored in the workspace, and their associated resources, artifacts, and history live under the workspace. The fact that all these resources, artifacts, and history live under the workspace is a critical detail because the workspace is a kind of high-order container for all the models, experiments, and activity like experiment runs that we perform in Azure Machine Learning. Here is a list of resources associated with a workspace:

- **Azure Storage Account**   Stores machine learning artifacts such as job logs and Jupyter notebooks used with compute instances.
- **Azure Container Registry**   Stores created Docker containers when building custom environments.
- **Azure Application Insights**   Monitors and collects diagnostic information from inference endpoints.
- **Azure Key Vault**   Stores secrets used by compute targets and other sensitive information needed by the workspace.

> **NOTE   USING AN AZURE ML COMPUTE IN A JUPYTER NOTEBOOK**
>
> When using an Azure ML compute in a Jupyter notebook, validate that web socket communication isn't disabled. Ensure your network allows websocket connections to *.instances.azureml.net and *.instances.azureml.ms.

> **IMPORTANT   BEWARE OF CREATING SUB-RESOURCES WHEN CREATING A COMPUTER CLUSTER**
>
> Creating compute clusters and instances in Azure Machine Learning generates sub-resources like VMs, load balancers, virtual networks, and bandwidth.

In the next section, we will look at developer tools for interacting with the workspace. This should provide you with a better understanding of how you can create jobs or experiments in the workspace using a variety of tools. We will also introduce the Python SDK v2.0, which is important to understand. The objects the SDK provides will give you a deeper understanding of how Azure Machine Learning works and will allow you to perform tasks programmatically.

Installing and interacting with the Python SDK v2.0

The Azure Machine Learning SDK primarily supports Python, which is the most commonly used language for machine learning and data science projects. While there is no official SDK for other languages, you can interact with Azure Machine Learning services using REST APIs, which allow for integration with applications written in different programming languages.

To download and install the Azure Machine Learning SDK, visit the official Azure Machine Learning SDK documentation. For detailed information on the differences between SDK versions and language support, refer to the same documentation. However, the default install can be done using pip, the Python package manager (see Listing 1-1).

LISTING 1-1 Installing the Azure ML core library in Python

```
pip install azureml-core

#You can import this package and check the version with

import azureml.core
print(azureml.core.VERSION)
```

You can install additional packages that provide other features that are not included in the core package. For example, `azureml-automl-core` contains the core automated machine learning packages used by `azureml-train-automl` classes.

NEED MORE REVIEW? **INSTALLING THE SDK REVIEW**

You can read more about installing the SDK at *https://learn.microsoft.com/en-us/python/api/overview/azure/ml/install*

If you're building a machine learning solution in Azure, you will have to interact with the workspace at some point. You can interact with your Azure Machine Learning workspace using various developer tools such as the Azure Machine Learning SDK for Python, Azure CLI, or Visual Studio Code extension. For example, to access your workspace using the Python SDK, see Listing 1-2 for syntax.

LISTING 1-2 Creating a workspace using the Python SDK

```
Importing Workspace class from Azure ML core
from azureml.core import Workspace
ws = Workspace.get(name="your-workspace-name",
subscription_id="your-subscription-id",
resource_group="your-resource-group")
```

IMPORTANT **THE AZURE SDK COMES IN TWO MAJOR VERSIONS: 1.0 AND 2.0.**

Version 2.0 is the latest iteration and offers a more streamlined and simplified user experience compared to version 1.0. Key differences include a more intuitive API structure, enhanced integration with other Azure services, and improved performance. It's important to choose the version that best aligns with your project requirements and existing workflows.

Connecting to the workspace

Once you are comfortable, you can connect to the workspace for several tasks, including managing experiments or registering datasets. Although we will cover some of these tasks in more depth in another section, here are some samples to help you become familiar with the syntax. Feel free to try some of this sample code yourself (see Listing 1-3).

LISTING 1-3 Demo of several common MLOps tasks in the Azure Machine Learning SDK

```
from azureml.core import Workspace
ws = Workspace.from_config() # Reads config.json file

#Creating and Managing Experiments:
from azureml.core import Experiment
experiment = Experiment(workspace=ws, name='my_experiment')

#Registering and Retrieving Datasets:
from azureml.core import Dataset
datastore = ws.get_default_datastore()
dataset = Dataset.File.from_files((datastore, 'path/to/data'))
registered_dataset = dataset.register(workspace=ws, name='my_dataset')
retrieved_dataset = Dataset.get_by_name(workspace=ws, name='my_dataset', version='latest')

#Deploying Models:
model = ws.models['my_model']
service = model.deploy(workspace=ws, name='my_service', inference_config=infe
```

There is another way to interact with the SDK, and that is through the Azure CLI. If you are more comfortable with scripting in Powershell or Bash, you might prefer the Azure CLI.

Using the Azure CLI (v2)

The Azure CLI (v2) offers a command-line interface for managing Azure Machine Learning resources. We can show some of the most frequent tasks for interacting with the workspace using the Azure CLI (see Listing 1-4).

LISTING 1-4 MLOps tasks using the Azure CLI (v2) instead of the SDK

```
#Creating a Workspace:
az ml workspace create --name myworkspace --resource-group myresourcegroup

# Submitting Experiments:
az ml job create --file experiment.yml

#Registering Datasets:
az ml data create --file dataset.yml

#Deploying Models:
az ml model deploy --name myservice --model mymodel:1
```

Azure Machine Learning Studio, CLI, SDK, and other integrations

Azure Machine Learning Studio is a GUI option for interacting with Azure Machine Learning services and designing a data science solution in Azure. We can compare Azure Machine

Learning Studio with other options for interacting with Azure Machine Learning services like the CLI and SDK.

The best way to compare the options is to first determine your use case. If you use case requires you to interact programmatically with machine learning services, for example, because you need to automate some steps in your workflow like model training and you want to have full access to all the features the SDK provides, then you might consider the SDK or CLI.

Choosing between the SDK and the CLI

With both the Azure CLI and the Python SDK available, which should you choose? While you can package up Azure CLI commands and build an Azure DevOps continuous integration pipeline to automate many of your model operations, on the other hand, if you need to interact with compute, models, and storage in the workspace and want to use Python, then the SDK is a better option. In other scenarios, the choice may not be clear, but there are a few considerations:

- **Authentication** You should ensure proper authentication when using the SDK or CLI, typically through Azure Active Directory or service principals.
- **Version Control** It is best practice to integrate with Git for version control of machine learning projects and code.
- **Collaboration** Share workspaces and resources with team members to facilitate collaboration.

In the next section, we will look at version control for our code. This will involve understanding Git and how to integrate it with the workspace and is an essential part of developing a data science solution in Azure.

Set up Git integration for source control

Integrating Git with your Azure Machine Learning workspace allows for efficient version control and collaboration on machine learning projects. This integration enables you to track changes, manage code, and collaborate with team members using a familiar source control system.

> **IMPORTANT** **USE GIT-MANAGED VERSION CONTROL FOR SOURCE CODE**
>
> There are also data version control systems for data—for example, the open-source DVC (data version control) project under the Apache 2.0 license is a project you might hear about in the real world. DVC has many commands similar to Git for versioning data, but there are specific features in Azure Machine Learning called Datasets that allow you to version data.

Git is a widely used version control system that enables collaboration and sharing of projects. Azure Machine Learning (AML) offers comprehensive support for Git repositories, allowing you to track your work efficiently (see Figure 1-6). You can clone repositories directly onto your shared workspace file system, utilize Git on your local workstation, or incorporate Git into your CI/CD pipeline. When submitting a job to AML, if the source files are stored in a local Git repository, the system tracks information about the repository as part of the training process. This feature is not limited to any specific central repository, so you can use repositories cloned from various services like GitHub, GitLab, Bitbucket, Azure DevOps, or any other Git-compatible service.

To enhance your experience with Git, you can use Visual Studio Code, which provides a graphical user interface for interacting with Git. For those working with Azure Machine Learning, Visual Studio Code can be integrated with AML remote compute instances. Additionally, AML provides a shared file system for all users in the workspace, allowing you to clone Git repositories into this file share. It is recommended to clone the repository into your user directory to avoid conflicts with other users. To do this, you can create a compute instance and open a terminal within the AML workspace, where you'll have access to a full Git client and can manage your repositories using the Git CLI experience.

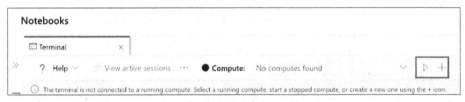

FIGURE 1-6 Setting up Git integration in an Azure Machine Learning workspace

---

NEED MORE REVIEW? **GIT INTEGRATION FOR MACHINE LEARNING TRAINING**

You can read more about machine learning training and Git integration. Additional info is available at *https://learn.microsoft.com/en-us/azure/machine-learning/ concept-train-model-git-integration*

While we can connect to Git and make use of version control in our project, it might not be clear at this point what the benefits are, but there are several—with reproducibility being the most important. Data science requires reproducible experiments; this is part of the scientific method, and there are several best practices including using source control that contribute to making your experiments reproduce.

IMPORTANT **EXPERIMENT REPRODUCIBILITY IN DESIGNING AN AZURE SOLUTION**

A reproducible experiment in Azure Machine Learning refers to the ability for one data scientist to reproduce the results or output of an experiment created by another data scientist. This requires source control (the original code) but also the data (features that were used to train the model), configuration, and other artifacts that were originally used in the experiment.

Benefits of Git integration

There are several benefits to integrating Git into your process when building a data science solution on Azure. The most important benefit beyond version control is reproducibility. The scientific method requires reproducibility in experiments, and maintaining a history of your project's experiments—including metrics, models, and other artifacts like snapshots of your training and validation datasets—feeds into reproducibility. Several benefits are listed below:

- **Version Control**   Track changes to your machine learning code and experiments over time.
- **Collaboration**   Collaborate with team members by sharing code and managing merge conflicts.
- **Reproducibility**   Maintain a history of your project's evolution, ensuring that experiments are reproducible.

In the real world, there are several scenarios where you might want to use version control. It is not enough just to know that you need version control or even why you need it (for example, to make your experiments reproducible) but you should be able to identify specific scenarios where version control is used. We can list some of these scenarios as follows:

- **New Data Availability**   When new data is available for retraining models.
- **Data Preparation Changes**   When applying different data preparation or feature engineering approaches.
- **Prerequisites**   Azure Machine Learning SDK for Python, including the `azureml-datasets` package. An Azure Machine Learning workspace.
- **Registering and Retrieving Dataset Versions**   Registering a Dataset Version: Use the `register()` method with the `create_new_version` parameter set to `True` to register a new version of a dataset. If no existing dataset is registered, a new dataset is created with version 1.
- **Retrieving a Dataset by Name**   Use the `Dataset.get_by_name()` method to retrieve the latest version of a dataset or specify the version parameter to retrieve a specific version.
- **Versioning Best Practices**   Single Source of Truth: Datasets in Azure Machine Learning are references to data in your storage service, ensuring a single source of truth managed by your storage service.
- **Immutability**   Avoid modifying data content referenced by a dataset version. Save new data in a separate folder and create a new dataset version to include data from that new folder.

In the next section, we will deep dive into managing data in the Azure Machine Learning workspace, starting with some of the low-level details of how data is stored and how you can bring data into your experiments and pipelines by using datasets.

Skill 1.3: Manage data in an Azure Machine Learning workspace

We have discussed the management of compute resources and environments for machine learning use cases, but designing solutions for machine learning requires skills to manage data. The exam covers the management of data in Azure Machine Learning, so knowledge of how to select Azure storage resources and use these storage resources to register and maintain datastores are the cornerstone of data management in Azure Machine Learning as well as more advanced concepts like data assets.

> **This skill covers how to:**
> - Select Azure storage resources
> - Register and maintain datastores
> - Create and manage data assets

Select Azure storage resources

You already know that the workspace itself is the top-level resource for Azure Machine Learning (see Figure 1-7 for a visualization of this hierarchy); however, you can interact with other resources in Azure. We've also discussed compute targets and how you can select compute, but you can do the same with storage, and if you work with big data, you can even interact with Azure storage resources like Azure Data Lake Storage Gen2 for big data analytics workloads. We already know how important it is to select compute targets based on your workloads, but the same is true for selecting storage resources.

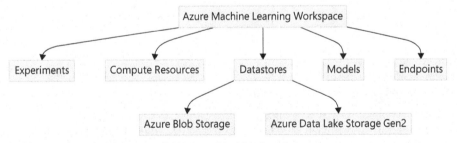

FIGURE 1-7 Hierarchy of resources in an Azure Machine Learning workspace

In the simplest scenario, when you have a small amount of data you can import data from a local machine (for example, tabular data in a CSV format containing sales data for use in an experiment) or an Azure storage resource. Continuing with this example, if you had several years or months of sales data partitioned by year, month, and day (this is a common pattern you will see when storing time series), you might store it in Azure Data Lake Storage in a container called sales.

Azure Machine Learning allows you to connect to your data without having to import it directly (remember, moving data is expensive, and we would like to minimize data movement). The reason why moving data is expensive is that copying data takes processing time and requires physical memory to load data, and if you're sending the data over a network, your solution needs to account for this additional latency—especially if you are working in a big data scenario with high data volumes. So, you might ask what kind of Azure storage resources are available to select in your workspace.

When selecting Azure storage resources for your Azure Machine Learning workspace, consider the following options:

- **Azure Blob Storage** Ideal for storing large volumes of unstructured data, such as images, text, and binary data. It's cost effective for storing data used in machine learning experiments and training. It is worth understanding orders of magnitude when sizing large volumes of data. For example, if your solution needs to support 100 users, and each user generates 10 GB of data, then you need to plan to store 1000 GB, or 1 TB, of data. You should also anticipate future growth and add some buffer room, so if you expect growth to double or triple in the next few years, you could plan to use several terabytes. Since Azure storage can accommodate petabytes of data, we have validated our solution storage requirements.

- **Azure Data Lake Storage** Suitable for big data analytics, as it provides a hierarchical file system and supports large-scale data processing. It's useful for machine learning projects that require data lake capabilities.

You should choose the storage option that best fits your data size, structure, and access patterns. Figure 1-8 shows several options available for Azure storage.

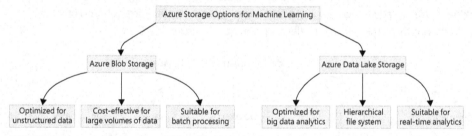

FIGURE 1-8 Azure storage options for machine learning

You might notice that the URI (uniform resource identifier) is used for representing a storage location. These long strings have a pattern to them; they include a protocol and information about the underlying datastore including the path and format, and it is important to understand what the URI looks like for different storage locations since in a real-world scenario you may have to use these URIs for connecting to storage (see Table 1-6).

TABLE 1-6 URIs for various Azure storage services

Storage	URI
Azure Machine Learning Datastore	`azureml://datastores/<data_store_name>/paths/<folder1>/<folder2>/` `<folder3>/<file>.parquet`
Local Computer	`./home/username/data/my_data`
Public http(s) Server	`https://raw.githubusercontent.com/pandas-dev/pandas/main/doc/` `data/titanic.csv`
Blob Storage	`wasbs://<containername>@<accountname>.blob.core.windows.` `net/<folder>/`
Azure Data Lake (gen2)	`abfss://<file_system>@<account_name>.dfs.core.windows.` `net/<folder>/<file>.csv`
Azure Data Lake	`adl://<accountname>.azuredatalakestore.net/<folder1>/<folder2>`

A uniform resource identifier (URI) in Azure Machine Learning represents a storage location, which can be on your local computer, Azure storage, or a publicly available http(s) location. URIs play a crucial role in specifying data locations for Azure Machine Learning jobs.

Understanding the use of URIs and their modes in Azure Machine Learning can help you effectively manage data storage and access for your machine learning jobs, ensuring efficient data handling and security. Some of the low-level details of interacting with Azure storage in an Azure Machine Learning workspace can be turned into a mental map of higher-level abstractions that are highly useful in designing data science solutions in Azure. One of these abstractions is known as the *datastore*.

It is also worth noting that you should choose https and abfss protocols (note that the s at the end means TLS 1.3 enabled) providing encryption during transport over http or abfs (in fact, protocols without TLS enabled are not suitable for production). Also be aware of any deprecation notices in the Azure documentation—for example, specific computes like Databricks that might be used within Azure Machine Learning can require use of a specific URI for mounting storage, while others may be depreciated.

Register and maintain datastores

In Azure Machine Learning, datastores provide a convenient way to connect to various Azure storage services, enabling efficient data management and security in machine learning projects. If you are familiar with tools like Azure Data Factory, datastores are similar to linked services in that they point to an underlying store that could be a database or data lake (they can also be things like file shares, but these should be used with caution when designing a data science solution, especially for big data scenarios). Selecting the appropriate storage and authentication method is crucial for optimizing data access and maintaining data security.

Benefits of an Azure Machine Learning datastore include the following features. Figure 1-9 shows how to create a new datastore.

- Unified API: Offers a common API for interacting with different storage types (Blob, Files, ADLS), simplifying data access.

- Easier Discovery: Facilitates the discovery of useful datastores in team operations, enhancing collaboration and efficiency.

- Secures connection information for credential-based access (service principal, SAS, key), eliminating the need to include sensitive information in scripts.

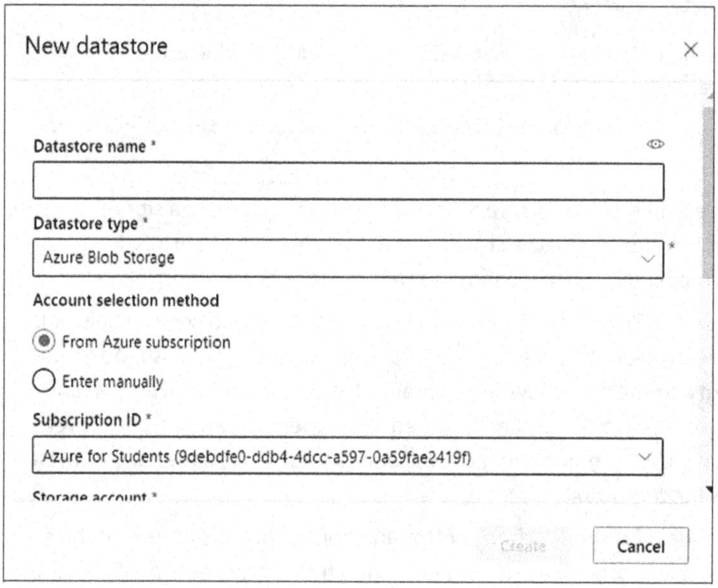

FIGURE 1-9 Creating a storage layer API

Once registered, datastores can be accessed in your machine learning experiments and pipelines for reading and writing data and provide encryption at rest. You can also manage datastores by updating connection information, authentication methods, or deleting unused datastores. Look at the example code in Listing 1-5 to understand how to work with datastores.

LISTING 1-5 Creating datastores in Azure ML SDK

```
#Registering a Blob storage datastore:
from azureml.core import Workspace, Datastore
ws = Workspace.from_config()
blob_datastore = Datastore.register_azure_blob_container(
workspace=ws,
datastore_name='my_blob_datastore',
container_name='mycontainer',
account_name='myaccount',
account_key='myaccountkey'
)
```

A security concern when designing a solution in Azure is that you should not store account keys and other sensitive information in code; instead, use an Azure Key Vault. Understanding the benefits and usage of datastores in Azure Machine Learning allows you to effectively manage your data storage and access, ensuring seamless data integration in data science projects.

Create and manage data assets

In the design of data science solutions, effective data management is crucial. Azure Machine Learning provides robust tools for handling data through datasets and dataflows, the two types of data assets available. Datasets ensure that data used for training and inference is accessible and manageable, while dataflows enable systematic preprocessing of data. These components are essential for developing scalable, reproducible, and efficient machine learning models. Here are some use cases of data flows:

- **Data Preprocessing** Dataflows are used to clean, transform, and normalize data, ensuring that it meets the requirements of various machine learning algorithms.

- **Multi-Model Deployment** In scenarios where multiple models are deployed, dataflows ensure that each model receives data in the correct format and structure.

Creating datasets in Azure Machine Learning

In Azure Machine Learning, datasets and datastores are two distinct concepts that are often used together but serve different purposes. A *datastore* is a storage abstraction that provides a mechanism to connect to and manage data in various storage services like Azure Blob Storage, Azure Data Lake, or Azure SQL Database. It acts as a bridge between your Azure Machine Learning workspace and the underlying storage service.

On the other hand, a *dataset* is a reference to a specific set of data that can be used in experiments and training models. Datasets are created from datastores and provide a way to version, track, and manage the data used in machine learning workflows. While a datastore points to the entire storage container or database, a dataset points to a specific subset of data within that storage, such as a file, folder, or table. Listing 1-6 is a code snippet showing how to create a dataset using the SDK.

LISTING 1-6 Creating a dataset in the SDK

```
from azureml.core.dataset import Dataset
# Create a tabular dataset from a CSV file in the datastore
csv_path = [(datastore, 'path/to/your/csvfile.csv')]
tabular_dataset = Dataset.Tabular.from_delimited_files(path=csv_path)

# Register the dataset in the workspace
tabular_dataset = tabular_dataset.register(workspace=ws,
name='My Tabular Dataset',
description='A sample tabular dataset')
```

Datasets in Azure Machine Learning support versioning, which allows you to track changes in your data over time and ensure reproducibility in your experiments. When you register a dataset, you can specify a version, and Azure ML will maintain a history of all versions. You can retrieve a specific version of a dataset by using the `get_by_name` method with the version parameter.

Tracking data in experiments

We now have enough knowledge to put all the pieces together and see how we can track data in experiments. This is kind of a preview of what is to come in Chapter 2, but for now you should be aware that Azure Machine Learning tracks your data as input and output datasets throughout your experiment:

- **Input Datasets**   Tracked as a `DatasetConsumptionConfig` object or when your script calls specific methods like `get_by_name()` or `get_by_id()`.
- **Output Datasets**   Tracked when you pass an `OutputFileDatasetConfig` object or register a dataset in your script.

You can use the `run.get_details()` method (this code can be called inside of a notebook) to track the input datasets used with the experiment run. Registered models can also be associated with datasets, allowing you to see which models are registered with a specific dataset.

In the final skill of this chapter, we will go beyond our understanding of selecting compute for a workload and look at how we can manage compute targets in the workspace, including creating compute targets once we know what kind of compute we require and how to use them in an experiment. We also look at technical topics of Apache Spark pools and get into some of the details on fine-tuning these in Azure Machine Learning.

Skill 1.4: Manage compute for experiments in Azure Machine Learning

Managing compute for experiments in Azure Machine Learning involves creating compute targets for experiments and model training, selecting environments that provide a way to manage dependencies like Python packages, and package versions that match a particular machine learning use case.

This skill covers how to:
- Create compute targets for experiments and training
- Select an environment for a machine learning use case
- Configure attached compute resources, including Apache Spark pools
- Monitor compute utilization

Create compute targets for experiments and training

Selecting the appropriate compute target for experiments and training is a critical step in the Azure Machine Learning workflow. While we have already talked about evaluating compute to match workloads and the types of compute targets available, you also need to know how to create a compute target. This section provides more details on choosing specific compute targets for experiments, both through the Azure Machine Learning Studio UI and the Python SDK.

Creating compute targets

In Azure Machine Learning (AML), compute targets are a crucial abstraction that encapsulates the concept of a compute resource. We've seen before when talking about selecting compute for our workload that these resources can vary from your local machine to a cluster of Azure virtual machines (VMs) or even an Apache Spark pool, providing the flexibility to choose the appropriate compute power for your machine learning tasks.

To interact with compute targets, you can use the Azure Machine Learning Python SDK. Here's how you can get started: To retrieve an existing compute target within a workspace ws, you can use the following code:

```
from azureml.core import ComputeTarget
target = ComputeTarget(ws, '<compute_target_name>')
```

To get a list of all compute targets within a workspace ws, you can use:

```
#List Existing Compute Targets:
ComputeTarget.list(ws)
```

Before submitting a job, it's common to check the available compute resources in a workspace, especially if you are working within a team. This can be easily done through Azure ML Studio.

> **NEED MORE REVIEW?** **CREATING A COMPUTE TARGET**
>
> You can read more about the official Microsoft cheat sheet for creating compute targets at https://azure.github.io/azureml-cheatsheets/docs/cheatsheets/python/v1/compute-targets/

Creating a new compute target is straightforward and can be done via Azure ML Studio:

1. Navigate to the Compute menu and click the Compute Clusters tab.
2. Click the New (+) button to start the creation process.
3. Fill in the required information, such as the compute name, virtual machine type, priority, size, and scaling settings.
4. For more advanced configurations, you can enable SSH access on your compute target by providing the admin username, password, and SSH key.

When designing an Azure solution, you must consider cost effectiveness, and one way to make the solution more cost effective is to choose low-priority compute targets. These are a cost-effective option similar to Databricks spot instances, but they do not guarantee the availability of compute nodes. Your job may be preempted if there's a higher priority demand for resources.

If you prefer to create compute targets programmatically, you can use the Azure ML Python SDK (see Listing 1-7).

LISTING 1-7 Idempotent compute target script

```
from azureml.core import Workspace
from azureml.core.compute import ComputeTarget, AmlCompute
from azureml.core.compute_target import ComputeTargetException
ws = Workspace.from_config() # Automatically looks for an .azureml directory
cpu_cluster_name = "cpu-cluster"
# Verify whether the cluster already exists
try:
    cpu_cluster = ComputeTarget(workspace=ws, name=cpu_cluster_name)
    print('Found existing cluster, using it.')
except ComputeTargetException:
    compute_config = AmlCompute.provisioning_configuration(vm_size='STANDARD_D2_V2',
_nodes=4,
idle_seconds_before_scaledown=2400)
    cpu_cluster = ComputeTarget.create(ws, cpu_cluster_name, compute_config)
cpu_cluster.wait_for_completion(show_output=True)
```

This is a big block of code, so let's break it down. The code snippet checks whether a compute target with the specified name exists and creates it if it does not exist. This logic is a common pattern for working with compute targets because it establishes a property called *idempotence* with which you can run the code more than once without errors. You can also configure the VM size, maximum number of nodes, and idle time before scale-down according to your workload requirements.

Compute targets in Azure Machine Learning provide a flexible way to manage your compute resources, whether you're working on a local machine or leveraging the power of Azure VMs. If you understand how to create and manage these targets, you can optimize your machine learning workflows for efficiency and cost effectiveness. In the next section, we'll look at compute targets for experiments.

Selecting a compute target for an experiment in Azure Machine Learning Studio UI

You can follow this step-by-step procedure for selecting a compute target for an experiment (see Figure 1-10):

1. Navigate to Azure Machine Learning Studio: Open your Azure Machine Learning workspace in the Azure portal and click Launch Studio to open Azure Machine Learning Studio.

2. Create a New Experiment: Go to the Experiments section in the left navigation pane and select New Experiment.

3. Configure Experiment Settings: Enter a name for your experiment and select the dataset you want to use.

4. Select the Compute option in the experiment settings.

5. Choose an existing compute target from the list or create a new one by clicking New and configuring the compute resources.

6. Save your settings after selecting the compute target.

FIGURE 1-10 Creating a compute target for Azure Machine Learning

EXAM TIP

Understand the different types of compute targets available in Azure Machine Learning and their use cases. Familiarize yourself with the process of creating and configuring compute targets both in the Azure ML Studio UI and by using the Python SDK (we'll cover this in the next section).

Selecting a compute target for an experiment using Azure Machine Learning Python SDK

You'll find that you can do many of the same things in the UI that you can in the SDK (in fact, the SDK is more flexible and allows more control over your solution, so you should think carefully about the limitations of the UI and when you may need to use the SDK). In particular, once you've defined your compute target, you can select it by name and use it in an experiment. See the code snippet in Listing 1-8.

LISTING 1-8 Selecting compute targets for an experiment

```
compute_target = ws.compute_targets['your-compute-target-name']
src = ScriptRunConfig(source_directory='your-source-directory',
 script='your-training-script.py',
 compute_target=compute_target,
environment=environment)
run = experiment.submit(config=src)
run.wait_for_completion(show_output=True)
```

You probably noticed in the above code snippet that we left something out of the experiment. In the next section, we'll explain what an experiment is and how you can use them for your machine learning use case.

Select an environment for a machine learning use case

Where does our code run? Packages and runtime dependencies are needed to interact with the outside world. An environment in Azure Machine Learning encapsulates the settings and dependencies required for training and scoring machine learning models. It includes Python packages, Docker images, environment variables, and software settings. Let's look at how we can create environments.

Creating an environment

You can create a custom environment by specifying the necessary Python packages, Docker image, and other settings. If you require custom R binaries from CRAN, you can use Docker images (but be aware of security patches and optimizing the size of your image). Since Docker images require hosting in a container registry, you might be interested in using a curated environment instead that suits your use case.

Alternatively, you can use a curated environment provided by Azure Machine Learning. Curated environments are predefined and optimized for common machine learning scenarios.

Using a curated environment

Curated environments are available by default in your workspace and are backed by cached Docker images, which reduce job preparation time. To use a curated environment, you can retrieve it by name from your workspace. For example, to use the AzureML-Minimal environment:

```
from azureml.core import Workspace, Environment
ws = Workspace.from_config()
myenv = Environment.get(workspace=ws, name="AzureML-Minimal")
```

Understanding the concept of environments in Azure Machine Learning also plays a role in ensuring reproducibility and consistency across training and scoring runs. Familiarize yourself with the process of creating custom environments and using curated environments for different machine learning tasks.

> **NEED MORE REVIEW?** **ENVIRONMENTS AND THEIR ROLE IN REPRODUCIBLE EXPERIMENTS**
>
> You can read about curated environments in the official documentation for Azure Machine Learning here: *https://learn.microsoft.com/en-us/azure/machine-learning/how-to-use-environments?view=azureml-api-1#use-a-curated-environment*

The following code snippet shows how to create an environment and register it with a private registry:

```
env = Environment('<env-name>')
env.docker.base_image = "/my/private/img:tag" # image repository path
env.docker.base_image_registry.address = "myprivateacr.azurecr.io" # private registry
# Retrieve username and password from the workspace key vault
env.docker.base_image_registry.username = ws.get_default_keyvault().
get_secret("username")
env.docker.base_image_registry.password = ws.get_default_keyvault().
get_secret("password")
```

Choosing the right environment is critical for the successful execution of machine learning experiments, especially when working with remote compute targets. Always verify that the environment you select meets the requirements of your machine learning project in terms of dependencies and settings. Figure 1-11 shows selecting an environment.

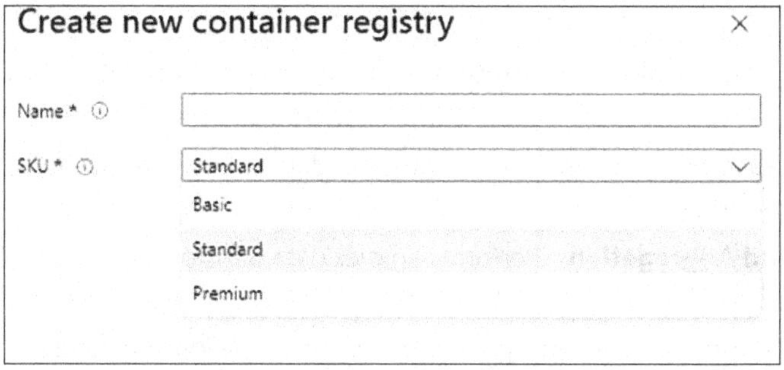

FIGURE 1-11 Container registries for hosting custom machine learning environments

In the next section, we'll look at a special kind of compute called *Apache Spark pools* for a distributed training scenario. This is an important concept when working with big data, and you will need to understand when to apply Apache Spark pools for distributed training over another strategy like batching or chunking your data into smaller pieces that fit into memory.

Configure attached compute resources, including Apache Spark pools

Azure Machine Learning integrates with Azure Synapse Analytics to provide access to distributed computation resources through Apache Spark (see Figure 1-12), enabling scalable data processing and machine learning workflows. Example use cases include:

- Large-scale data transformation
- Machine learning model training on big data
- Real-time data analytics

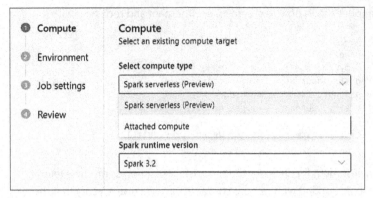

FIGURE 1-12 Architecture of Apache Spark integration in Azure Machine Learning

Why would you want to configure a Spark pool? There are several big data and machine learning use cases, including:

- **Real-Time Data Processing** Analyze streaming data in real time using Apache Spark's streaming capabilities.
- **Large-Scale Machine Learning** Train machine learning models on large datasets distributed across multiple nodes.
- **Data Transformation and Aggregation** Perform complex data transformations and aggregations on big datasets.

In the next section, we will deep-dive into specific procedures and information you need to know to configure Apache Spark pools to work with Azure Machine Learning for use in several use cases. We will look at serverless and attached Synapse configurations.

Configuring serverless Spark compute

The serverless Spark option offers a fully managed, on-demand Apache Spark compute cluster (see Figure 1-13), ideal for quick access to distributed computing resources for interactive Spark code development, batch job submissions, and running machine learning pipelines. There are a couple of advantages and disadvantages of this approach (as with any technical solution, there are trade-offs you must consider when evaluating a machine learning solution):

- Advantages include no dependencies on other Azure resources and simplified resource management.
- Disadvantages include the absence of a persistent Hive metastore and limited support for certain Spark utilities.

Configuring an attached synapse Spark pool

Apache Spark enables the use of a Spark pool created in Azure Synapse within the Azure Machine Learning workspace, suitable for reusing existing Synapse Spark pools and accessing native Azure Synapse features. Users are responsible for provisioning, attaching, configuring, and managing the Synapse Spark pool.

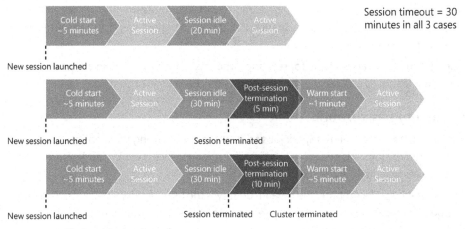

FIGURE 1-13 Lifetime of a Spark session

In Azure Machine Learning, configuring the Spark cluster size is a crucial step to ensure that your Apache Spark jobs have the necessary resources to run efficiently. Users can customize the Spark cluster size based on their specific workloads by adjusting the following parameters:

- **Number of Executors**   Executors are individual processes running on nodes in the Spark cluster. Each executor performs a portion of the overall task. Increasing the number of executors allows for parallel processing of larger datasets, thus reducing the overall execution time of Spark jobs.

- **Executor Cores**   This parameter specifies the number of CPU cores allocated to each executor. Allocating more cores per executor can improve the processing speed, especially for CPU-intensive tasks. However, it's essential to balance this with the available cores in your cluster to avoid resource contention.

- **Executor Memory**   This setting determines the amount of memory allocated to each executor. Memory-intensive operations, such as data shuffling and aggregation, require sufficient memory to avoid spilling data to disk, which can significantly slow down processing.

You can customize the Spark cluster size by specifying parameters such as the number of executors, executor cores, and executor memory to optimize resource allocation for your specific workload.

Configuring resource access for Spark jobs

In Azure Machine Learning, configuring resource access for Spark jobs is essential to ensure that your jobs can securely access the data and resources they need. Spark jobs can utilize two primary methods for accessing resources: managed identity and user identity passthrough. The choice between these methods depends on your security requirements and the specific setup of your Azure environment.

A managed identity is an Azure Active Directory identity that is managed automatically by Azure. It is used to authenticate services and resources without storing credentials in the code.

For serverless Spark compute, the managed identity is the compute identity of the serverless Spark pool. For attached Synapse Spark pools, it is the compute identity of the attached Synapse Spark pool.

Managed identities are suitable for scenarios where you want to maintain a separation between user identities and the identities used by services to access resources.

User identity passthrough

User identity passthrough allows Spark jobs to access resources using the identity of the user who submitted the job. This approach provides fine-grained access control and ensures that resource access is audited under the user's identity.

For serverless Spark compute, the default identity is the user identity. For attached Synapse Spark pools, user identity passthrough is used for interactive data wrangling in notebook sessions.

EXAM TIP

Be familiar with the advantages and disadvantages of serverless Spark compute and attached Synapse Spark pools. Understand how to define Spark cluster size and ensure resource access for optimal performance of Spark jobs in Azure Machine Learning.

The final section of this chapter will look at monitoring compute utilization, which is useful for many of the compute targets we have looked at including Spark pools, since monitoring provides observability and allows you to make more informed, data-driven decisions about cost optimization, scalability, and efficiency. It can also help you to gather data you need to make more informed decisions on how well your chosen compute is meeting your workload requirements.

Monitor compute utilization

Monitoring compute utilization is essential for optimizing resource usage and cost management in Azure Machine Learning. Effective monitoring helps you ensure that your compute resources are being used efficiently and allows you to make informed decisions about scaling and cost optimization. We can view utilization metrics and setting up alerts and notifications as a two-pronged strategy for monitoring compute in Azure Machine Learning.

View utilization metrics

Azure Machine Learning provides a comprehensive platform that not only enables you to train and deploy machine learning models but also offers tools to monitor the utilization of your compute targets. By keeping an eye on utilization metrics, you can gain valuable insights into how your resources are being used and make informed decisions. Here's a step-by-step guide to view the utilization metrics of your compute targets in Azure Machine Learning:

1. Access the Azure Portal or Azure Machine Learning Studio: Start by logging in to the Azure portal or directly accessing the Azure Machine Learning Studio.

2. Navigate to Compute Targets: Once in the Azure Machine Learning workspace, go to the Compute section, where you can see a list of your compute targets.

3. Select a Compute Target: Select the specific compute target for which you want to view the utilization metrics.

4. View Utilization Metrics: In the compute target, click the Monitoring (in preview) tab on the Details page, and you will find a section for utilization metrics including any jobs that have run in the time range selected. Here, you can see various metrics such as CPU usage, memory usage, and other resource utilization statistics (see Figure 1-14).

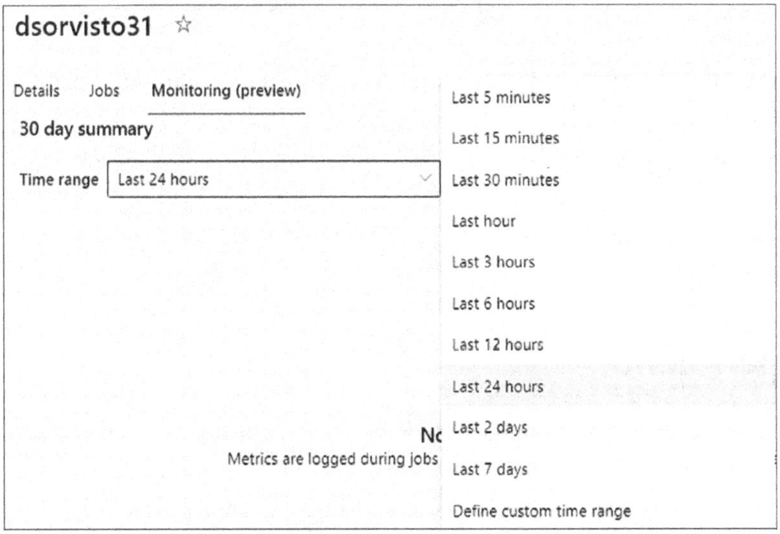

FIGURE 1-14 Selecting a time range to view metrics for a target compute

You can also configure alerts and notifications to monitor compute usage and detect anomalies. Alerts can be set up based on specific thresholds, such as CPU or memory usage exceeding a certain percentage, enabling you to take proactive measures to manage your resources if metrics deviate from an established baseline.

For more advanced monitoring and analysis, leverage the Azure Monitor service, which provides full-stack monitoring of applications, infrastructure, and networks in Azure, allowing you to collect telemetry data. Azure Monitor provides comprehensive monitoring capabilities, including log analytics, application insights, and more, allowing you to track and analyze compute resource usage over time.

Chapter summary

- You can determine the compute specifications and describe model deployment requirements, like CPU and memory for compute targets, based on your workload.

- You can manage Azure Machine Learning workspaces by first creating a workspace and then setting up integrations like Git.

- You can manage the data within a workspace like storage resources, registering and maintaining datastores for training data and creating data assets.

- You can manage compute resources for experiments and training. You can create compute targets , select environments for use in training and experiments, and configure attached resources. You can also monitor resource utilization with Azure monitor.

- You can choose between the Azure Machine Learning Studio and the Azure CLI and SDK, and you can decide which option best meets your use case.

- You can use Azure storage including Azure Data Lake Storage Gen2 to meet storage requirements. You also learned the difference between Azure Data Lake Storage and Azure Blob Storage.

- You can define a job and create jobs for training steps and use them within your solution to automate the execution of code on Azure resources.

- You can create Spark pools and use Spark to scale your solution when working with big data.

- You learned security concepts like user identity passthrough and can build solutions that support many users.

Thought experiment

In this thought experiment, demonstrate your skills and knowledge of the topics covered in this chapter. You can find the answers in the section that follows.

1. If you need to use a GPU-based VM like the Standard_NC6 for training in Azure Machine Learning, and no workspace currently exists, what is the first step you should take?

    A. Create a new Azure Machine Learning workspace.

    B. Directly purchase a Standard_NC6 VM.

    C. Configure a local machine with similar specifications.

    D. Ignore the requirement and use a CPU-based VM.

2. In an Azure Machine Learning workspace, when setting up a new environment for a machine learning project that involves deep learning for image classification, which of the following environments would be most appropriate?

    A. Python 3.6 with TensorFlow and Keras

    B. R with caret and randomForest

    C. Python 3.8 with PyTorch and scikit-learn

    D. Java with Deeplearning4j

3. How should you organize and manage your data assets in the Azure Machine Learning workspace to effectively handle training, testing, and validation sets while incorporating data versioning?

   A. Store all data in a single dataset without versioning.

   B. Use separate folders for each dataset without versioning.

   C. Create separate datasets for training, testing, and validation with version control.

   D. Focus only on training data and ignore versioning for simplicity.

Thought experiment answers

This section contains the solutions to the thought experiment. Each answer explains why the answer choice is correct.

1. The answer is **A**. Creating a new Azure Machine Learning workspace is the necessary first step if no workspace exists and you need to use a GPU-based VM like the Standard_NC6 for training. Options B, C, and D do not address the initial requirement of establishing a workspace in Azure Machine Learning, which is essential before any computational resource can be allocated.

2. The answer is **A**. Python 3.6 with TensorFlow and Keras is most appropriate for a deep learning project involving image classification in an Azure Machine Learning workspace. These libraries are specifically designed for deep learning tasks, making them the optimal choice. Options B and D use languages and tools not typically associated with deep learning for image classification, while Option C, though also viable with PyTorch, mentions Python 3.8, which is not as commonly paired with PyTorch for such tasks in workspace configurations.

3. The answer is **C**. Creating separate datasets for training, testing, and validation with version control is the best practice for organizing and managing data assets in an Azure Machine Learning workspace. This method allows for effective management of data lifecycle and ensures that each type of data is properly isolated and versioned for reproducibility and compliance. Options A, B, and D do not fully utilize the capabilities of Azure Machine Learning for managing data assets effectively, especially in regard to versioning and separation of datasets for different phases of machine learning projects.

CHAPTER 2

Explore data and train models

We're about to dive deep into the heart of the machine learning lifecycle: exploring data and training models. This chapter is designed to equip you with the skills and knowledge needed to handle data effectively and create optimized machine learning models using Azure Machine Learning.

Data exploration is the first step in any successful machine learning project. It's where you'll get to know your data, understand its characteristics, and prepare it for modeling. You'll learn how to access and wrangle data using Azure's data assets and datastores, making your data ready for the challenges ahead.

Model training is where the magic happens. You'll discover how to create models using the Azure Machine Learning Designer, leverage the power of automated machine learning for various data types, and even dive into custom model training using notebooks and Python SDKv2. We'll also cover hyperparameter tuning, a crucial step in optimizing your models for better performance.

By the end of this chapter, you'll have a solid understanding of how to explore data and train models in Azure Machine Learning, setting the stage for deploying and managing your models in the real world.

EXAM TIP

Follow the steps outlined in Skill 2.1 and Skill 2.2 to understand how to create models, data assets, and datastores in Azure Machine Learning Designer and by using the Python SDKv2. While you may prefer one over the other, pay close attention to the wording on the exam when a question asks about the Azure Machine Learning Designer or the SDK since it might impact how you answer the question.

Skills covered in this chapter:

- Skill 2.1: Explore data by using data assets and datastores
- Skill 2.2: Create models by using the Azure Machine Learning Designer
- Skill 2.3: Use automated machine learning to explore optimal models
- Skill 2.4: Use notebooks for custom model training
- Skill 2.5: Tune hyperparameters with Azure Machine Learning

As you journey through this chapter, remember that exploring data and training models are iterative processes. With each iteration, you'll gain deeper insights into your data and refine your models for better accuracy and performance. After acquiring the five skills in this chapter, you will be able to combine them to build training pipelines using automated machine learning and tune hyperparameters to iteratively improve the model performance using Azure Machine Learning.

Skill 2.1: Explore data by using data assets and datastores

In the process of developing a machine learning model, one of the first steps is exploring and understanding the data you're working with. Skill 2.1 focuses on the exploration of data using Azure Machine Learning's data assets and datastores. This skill is essential for data scientists and analysts who need to access, wrangle, and prepare data for model training. By mastering these techniques, you'll be able to create a solid foundation for building accurate and efficient machine learning models.

> **This skill covers how to:**
> - Access and wrangle data during interactive development
> - Wrangle interactive data with Apache Spark

Access and wrangle data during interactive development

In this section, you'll learn how to access data stored in Azure Machine Learning datastores and perform data wrangling operations interactively. This is crucial for exploratory data analysis and preprocessing steps before model training.

Imagine you're working on a project to predict customer churn based on historical transaction data. You need to access this data from an Azure Blob Storage, clean it, and perform feature engineering to prepare it for model training. You'll use Python in a Jupyter Notebook environment within Azure Machine Learning to load the data, handle missing values, encode categorical variables, and normalize numerical features.

> **NEED MORE REVIEW?**   **WRANGLING DATA IN AZURE MACHINE LEARNING**
>
> You can read more about wrangling data in Azure Machine learning at *https:// learn.microsoft.com/en-us/azure/machine-learning/how-to-access-data-interactives*

To demonstrate the end-to-end process of exploring data and training a model to predict customer churn using Azure Machine Learning, we'll go through the following steps:

1. Before you begin, make sure you have an Azure Machine Learning workspace set up. You can create one using the Azure portal or the Azure Machine Learning SDK. For detailed instructions, see the section "Manage an Azure Machine Learning workspace" in Chapter 1.

2. Create a datastore: Link your Azure Blob Storage account to your Azure Machine Learning workspace by creating a datastore. For a review of managing data in Azure Machine Learning, see Chapter 1, "Manage data in an Azure Machine Learning workspace." For convenience, here are the instructions for creating a datastore:

   1. Navigate to the Datastores section in the left menu and select the Datastores option under the Data section.

   2. Add a new datastore by clicking the New Datastore (+) button at the top of the Datastores page.

3. Access and explore data: Use the Azure Machine Learning SDK to access your data and perform exploratory data analysis (EDA) using Pandas.

4. Preprocess and prepare data: Clean the data, handle missing values, encode categorical variables, and normalize numerical features.

Listing 2-1 shows a sample code snippet that demonstrates these steps: Setting up your Azure Machine Learning workspace, creating and accessing a datastore, and preprocessing data. Next, we will show how to implement these steps using `Workspace` and `Datastore` objects.

LISTING 2-1 Implementing preprocessing steps needed to train a model

```
from azureml.core import Workspace, Datastore
import pandas as pd
from sklearn.model_selection import train_test_split
from sklearn.preprocessing import StandardScaler
from sklearn.linear_model import LogisticRegression
from sklearn.metrics import accuracy_score


# Set up your Azure Machine Learning workspace
subscription_id = 'your-subscription-id'
resource_group = 'your-resource-group'
workspace_name = 'your-workspace-name'
workspace = Workspace(subscription_id, resource_group, workspace_name)

# Create a datastore (if not already created)
datastore_name = 'your-datastore-name'
container_name = 'your-container-name'
account_name = 'your-storage-account-name'
datastore = Datastore.register_azure_blob_container(workspace=workspace,
datastore_name=datastore_name,
container_name=container_name,
account_name=account_name)
```

```
# Access data from the datastore
datastore_path = [(datastore, 'path/to/your/data.csv')]
data = Dataset.Tabular.from_delimited_files(path=datastore_path)
df = data.to_pandas_dataframe()

# Explore and preprocess the data (assuming 'Churn' is the target variable and it's a
binary classification problem)
df.fillna(df.mean(), inplace=True)  # Handle missing values
df = pd.get_dummies(df, drop_first=True)  # Encode categorical variables
X = df.drop('Churn', axis=1)
y = df['Churn']
X_train, X_test, y_train, y_test = train_test_split(X, y, test_size=0.3,
random_state=42)

# Normalize the data
scaler = StandardScaler()
X_train_scaled = scaler.fit_transform(X_train)
X_test_scaled = scaler.transform(X_test)

# Train a Logistic Regression model we imported
logreg = LogisticRegression()
logreg.fit(X_train_scaled, y_train)
# Predict on the test set
y_pred = logreg.predict(X_test_scaled)
# Evaluate the model
accuracy = accuracy_score(y_test, y_pred) print(f'Accuracy: {accuracy:.2f}')
```

In this example, we've used a logistic regression model for simplicity, but you can replace it with any other model suitable for your use case. Remember to adjust the data preprocessing steps according to the specific requirements of your dataset and the model you choose.

Wrangle interactive data with Apache Spark

Apache Spark is a powerful tool for handling large-scale data processing and analysis. In this topic, you'll explore how to use Apache Spark within Azure Machine Learning to wrangle data interactively.

Consider a scenario where you're dealing with a massive dataset of social media posts, and you need to perform sentiment analysis. The dataset is too large to process on a single machine, so you decide to use Apache Spark to process and clean the data in parallel. The decision to use Spark is reasonable if you have more than 20 GB of data, for example, where the data is too large to fit completely in memory on a single machine. You can also use Spark for much larger data volumes up to petabytes of data. You'll learn how to initialize a Spark session in Azure Machine Learning, read the data, and perform text preprocessing tasks like tokenization, stopword removal, and stemming. Figure 2-1 shows the workflow.

```
Start
   │
   ▼
Initialize Spark Session in Azure ML
   │
   ▼
Read Social Media Posts Data
   │
   ▼
Perform Tokenization
   │
   ▼
Remove Stopwords
   │
   ▼
Perform Stemming
   │
   ▼
Sentiment Analysis
   │
   ▼
End
```

FIGURE 2-1 Workflow for sentiment analysis solution in Apache Spark

To use Apache Spark pools within Azure Machine Learning for wrangling a large dataset of social media posts stored in a datastore, you can follow these steps, which include creating a Spark pool and creating a datastore.

1. Set Up Your Azure Machine Learning Workspace: Make sure you have an Azure Machine Learning workspace set up.

2. Create a Datastore: Link your Azure Blob Storage account (where your social media posts dataset is stored) to your Azure Machine Learning workspace by creating a datastore.

3. Create a Spark Pool: In the Azure portal, navigate to your Azure Synapse Analytics workspace and create a Spark pool. You can check to make sure the Spark pool is correctly configured by verifying the node count, node size, and other settings on the Spark pool configuration page.

If you followed the above instructions to configure your datastore and have created a Spark pool, then you are ready to use the Spark pool to read the large dataset from the datastore, perform text preprocessing tasks like tokenization, stopword removal, and stemming, and prepare the data for sentiment analysis. Before reading the code in Listing 2-2, you should have a conceptual understanding of Spark's execution model to understand how model training can be distributed using a feature like Spark pools. Figure 2-2 illustrates how Spark's execution model is built on the concept of a directed acyclic graph (DAG) internally.

Listing 2-2 demonstrates how to use the Spark pool to read the large dataset from the datastore, perform text preprocessing tasks like tokenization, stopword removal, and stemming, and prepare the data for sentiment analysis.

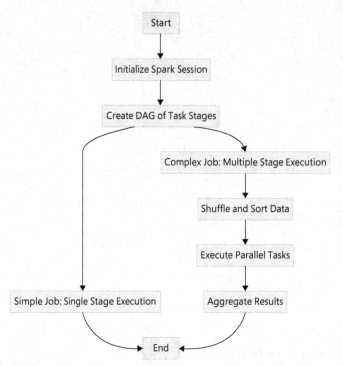

FIGURE 2-2 Workflow using Spark's directed acyclic graph (DAG) for task execution

LISTING 2-2 Spark pool for reading large datasets from the datastore and preprocessing tasks

```python
from azureml.core import Workspace, Datastore
from azureml.core.compute import SynapseCompute
from azureml.core.compute_target import ComputeTargetException
from pyspark.sql import SparkSession
from pyspark.ml.feature import Tokenizer, StopWordsRemover, HashingTF, IDF

# Set up your Azure Machine Learning workspace
subscription_id = 'your-subscription-id'
resource_group = 'your-resource-group'
workspace_name = 'your-workspace-name'
workspace = Workspace(subscription_id, resource_group, workspace_name)

# Create a Spark pool (if not already created)
spark_pool_name = "synapse-spark-pool"
try:
    spark_pool = SynapseCompute(workspace=workspace,
    name=spark_pool_name)
    print('Found existing Spark pool.')
except ComputeTargetException:
    print('Creating a new Spark pool.')
    spark_pool_config = SynapseCompute.
provisioning_configuration(compute_pool_name=spark_pool_name)
    spark_pool = ComputeTarget.create(workspace, spark_pool_name, spark_pool_config)
    spark_pool.wait_for_completion(show_output=True)
```

```
# Create a datastore (if not already created)
datastore_name = 'your-datastore-name'
container_name = 'your-container-name'
account_name = 'your-storage-account-name'
datastore = Datastore.register_azure_blob_container(workspace=workspace,
datastore_name=datastore_name,
container_name=container_name,
account_name=account_name)

# Initialize a Spark session
spark = SparkSession.builder.getOrCreate()

# Access data from the datastore
datastore_path = f"abfss://{container_name}@{account_name}.dfs.core.windows.net/path/to/
your/social_media_posts.csv"
data = spark.read.option("header", "true").csv(datastore_path)

# Preprocess the data
tokenizer = Tokenizer(inputCol="post", outputCol="tokens")
tokenized_data = tokenizer.transform(data)
remover = StopWordsRemover(inputCol="tokens", outputCol="filtered_tokens")
filtered_data = remover.transform(tokenized_data)
hashingTF = HashingTF(inputCol="filtered_tokens", outputCol="raw_features")
featurized_data = hashingTF.transform(filtered_data)
idf = IDF(inputCol="raw_features", outputCol="features")
idf_model = idf.fit(featurized_data)
final_data = idf_model.transform(featurized_data)
```

In this example, we used PySpark's `Tokenizer`, `StopWordsRemover`, `HashingTF`, and `IDF` to preprocess the text data. You can replace these with any other preprocessing steps suitable for your use case. After preprocessing, the `final_data` `DataFrame` (remember this is a Spark dataframe) will be ready for sentiment analysis or any other machine learning tasks.

Skill 2.2: Create models by using the Azure Machine Learning Designer

The Azure Machine Learning Designer enables you to create models for use in a training pipeline. In order to do this, we need to also be able to consume data assets such as training, validation, and test data in the Designer. These data assets can be used in the training pipeline, with inputs and outputs defined between steps. In this skill, you will develop the techniques and knowledge necessary to start building end-to-end data science solutions in Azure.

> **This skill covers how to:**
> - Create a training pipeline
> - Consume data assets from the Designer
> - Use custom code components in Designer
> - Evaluate the model, including responsible AI guidelines

Create a training pipeline

A training pipeline in Azure Machine Learning Designer is a sequence of steps to prepare data, train a model, and evaluate its performance. It provides a visual and modular approach to building machine learning workflows. We will first log in to the Azure portal, create a new Azure workspace, compute resources, and then design a pipeline:

1. Log in to the Azure portal and create a new Azure Machine Learning workspace with the necessary configurations.

2. Create compute resources.

3. Navigate to the Compute page in Azure Machine Learning Studio and set up a compute cluster for training your model.

4. Design Your Pipeline:

   a. Go to the Designer page and create a new pipeline (see Figure 2-3).

   b. Drag and drop modules onto the canvas to define your workflow, including data preprocessing, model training, and evaluation steps.

5. Configure and Run.

Set up the properties for each module, such as selecting the algorithm for the Train Model module and defining the evaluation metrics in the Evaluate Model module.

Submit the pipeline as an experiment and monitor its progress. Once the experiment is complete, examine the output of the Evaluate Model module to assess the performance of your trained model.

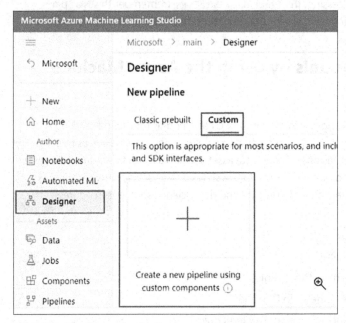

FIGURE 2-3 Creating a new pipeline

Consume data assets from the Designer

Data assets are important components of a training pipeline. They include datasets, data transformations, and data connections that are used throughout the pipeline to train and evaluate the model. You can use the Data page in Azure Machine Learning Studio to create new datasets or import existing ones. Supported data sources include web files, datastores, and local files.

Preprocessing data for model training

In the following steps, we will utilize modules to clean and transform data. Next, we will configure these modules to handle missing values and employ other modules to split data and eventually connect the final preprocessed data to our Train Model module for training. Here is a more detailed set of instructions you can follow on your own:

1. Utilize modules in Azure Machine Learning Studio such as Select Columns in Dataset and Normalize Data to clean and transform your data before training. The modules are in the module panel on the left side of the workspace, organized under category headings.

2. Configure these modules to select relevant features, handle missing values, and scale numerical data.

3. Employ the Split Data module to divide your dataset into training and validation sets.

4. Connect your preprocessed and split datasets to the Train Model module.

5. Ensure that the data flows correctly through the pipeline to provide the model with the necessary input for training.

Data assets form the backbone of a training pipeline in Azure Machine Learning Designer.

Proper management and utilization of these assets, from creation to preprocessing and splitting, are key to building an effective machine learning model.

Use custom code components in Designer

While Azure Machine Learning Designer provides a wide range of built-in modules, you may encounter scenarios where custom processing is required. Custom code components allow you to integrate Python or R scripts into your pipeline to perform specialized tasks.

Incorporating custom code

One way to use custom code in an Azure Machine Learning training pipeline is via a script. You can develop a Python or R script that performs the desired data processing or analysis task. For example, you might write a script to perform a unique data transformation or to generate custom features. More specifically, you can use the Execute Python Script module (see Figure 2-4). In the following steps, you will use an Execute Python Script module to upload your script and configure it. The configuration will involve both input and output ports. You can integrate this script module with the rest of your pipeline by connecting an output of a previous module with the input of this module, and the output of your script module with subsequent modules.

1. Add the Execute Python Script module to your pipeline in the Designer.

2. Upload your script to the module and configure any necessary input and output ports.

3. Connect the output of a previous module (e.g., data preprocessing) to the input of the Execute Python Script module.

4. Ensure that the output of your custom script is connected to subsequent modules for further processing or model training.

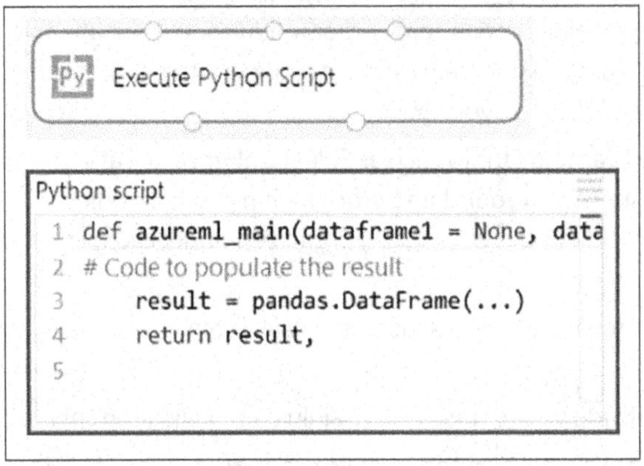

FIGURE 2-4 Using a custom Python script in Azure ML Designer

Notice that steps 3 and 4 are necessary to integrate your Python Script module with the rest of the pipeline, connecting output of the previous modules (which could itself be another data preprocessing step) to the input of your custom Python Script module (see Figure 2-5). Remember to connect the output of your custom module to the input of the next or subsequent module as well. It might seem obvious, but this is a subtle step because you can form DAGs (directed acyclic graphs) by connecting your module as inputs to many subsequent modules. The concept of a DAG is used when building pipelines that can have many parallel steps and can, for example, fan out. In addition to the fan-out pattern, a DAG can be used as a powerful abstraction for building sequential steps—steps that fan in or converge and manage parallelism and dependencies in your pipeline.

Run your pipeline to test the custom code component and, if necessary, iteratively refine it. Make any necessary adjustments to ensure that it performs as expected within the context of your workflow. Figure 2-5 shows how to connect inputs and outputs using a Python Script module.

Carefully configure each module in your pipeline. Double-check the parameters and settings to ensure they are appropriate for your data and the problem you're solving.

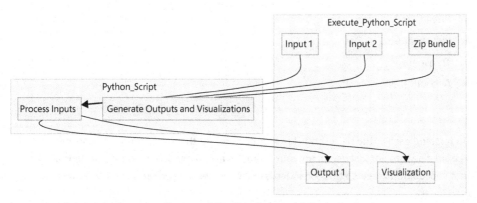

FIGURE 2-5 Connecting inputs and outputs in Python Script modules in the Designer

Verify that all modules are correctly connected in the pipeline. The output of one module should correctly feed into the input of the next. In the next section, we will look at a more robust procedure for evaluating the model and using responsible AI guidelines.

Evaluate the model, including responsible AI guidelines

Model evaluation is a critical step in the training pipeline. It helps you assess the performance of your model and ensure that it aligns with Responsible AI principles. Our first step is to understand how to evaluate the model using evaluation metrics.

Evaluation metrics

There is a module called the Evaluate Model. You can add this module to your pipeline after the training and scoring steps. This module provides various metrics such as accuracy, precision, recall, and F1 score to assess the performance of your classification model.

What does Evaluate Model do, and why should we use it? We can analyze the results of our models by examining the output of the Evaluate Model module to understand how well your model is performing.

> **IMPORTANT MODEL METRICS AND THEIR USES IN PIPELINES**
>
> Remember to pay attention to metrics that are particularly important for your specific use case and objectives.

Responsible AI considerations

Microsoft developed a standard called the Responsible AI Standard. This is a framework for building AI systems according to six principles:

- Model fairness
- Reliability and safety

- Privacy and security
- Inclusiveness
- Transparency
- Accountability

We can look at some of these principles in more detail and how we can practice the guidelines when designing our data science solutions in Azure by incorporating specific modules into our pipeline. Figure 2-6 illustrates the relationship between the responsible AI guidelines.

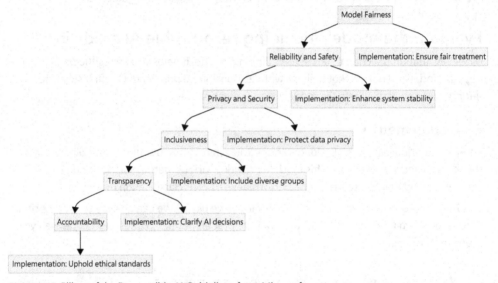

FIGURE 2-6 Pillars of the Responsible AI Guidelines from Microsoft

Fairness

When evaluating your model's predictions, it's important to integrate the fairness guideline to assess fairness across different demographic groups. This module helps detect any disparities and allows you to address them effectively, ensuring that your model maintains equity and avoids perpetuating biases. Considering demographic factors such as race or gender in prediction assessment provides valuable insights into potential biases, enabling proactive steps to mitigate them. This approach promotes inclusivity and fairness, which are fundamental principles in AI development and deployment.

Analyzing predictions through a demographic lens offers a deeper understanding of your model's performance. It helps uncover and rectify any underlying biases within your data or algorithm, ultimately leading to more just and reliable outcomes. Incorporating fairness into your evaluation process allows you to enhance the credibility and reliability of your model while promoting social responsibility in AI development. This approach increases the trust in your model's outputs but also contributes to creating a more equitable landscape in the applications where it's utilized.

Explainability

When exploring your model's predictions, using the Model Interpretability module provides insights into how the model makes decisions. This tool helps you understand the factors influencing these decisions, fostering transparency in the process. Transparency is key for stakeholders to grasp how the model reaches its conclusions, building trust and facilitating informed decision-making.

However, it's important to distinguish between model interpretability and fairness assessment. While interpretability focuses on understanding the model's decision-making process, fairness evaluation examines whether these predictions exhibit biases across different demographic groups. Both are vital for model evaluation, serving distinct purposes. Interpretability aids in comprehending how the model functions internally, while fairness assessment ensures equitable outcomes for all demographic groups. Thus, integrating both modules into your evaluation process offers a holistic view of your model's performance and its impact on diverse populations.

Privacy and security

Ensure that your model adheres to privacy and security guidelines, particularly when handling sensitive data. Implement appropriate measures to protect data confidentiality and integrity.

Incorporating custom code components in your training pipeline allows you to extend the functionality of Azure Machine Learning Designer with specialized processing tasks.

Evaluating your model with a focus on performance metrics and Responsible AI principles ensures that your model is not only accurate but also fair, transparent, and secure. Figure 2-7 illustrates the process of making decisions on model fairness.

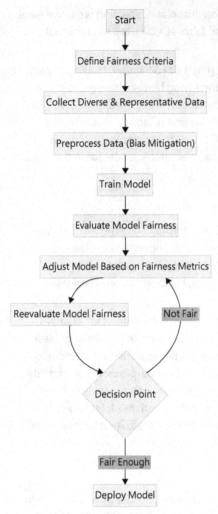

FIGURE 2-7 Ensuring model fairness in AI training

Skill 2.3: Use automated machine learning to explore optimal models

Azure Machine Learning service's automated ML capability is based on a breakthrough from the Microsoft Research division. It is distinct from competing solutions in the market. The approach combines ideas from collaborative filtering and Bayesian optimization. This combination allows it to search an enormous space of possible machine learning pipelines intelligently and efficiently. Essentially, it acts as a recommender system for machine learning pipelines. Just as streaming services recommend movies for users, automated ML recommends machine learning pipelines for datasets.

Use automated machine learning for tabular data

Imagine you're a data scientist working for a telecom company. Your task is to develop a machine learning model to predict customer churn based on various customer attributes. You decide to use Azure Machine Learning's Automated Machine Learning (AutoML) feature to quickly build and deploy the model. We'll break this down into setting up your environment, preparing your tabular data, and then using AutoML on your tabular data by looking at a real-world scenario.

Working with tabular data in Azure Machine Learning

This section covers how you can use objects like MLTable for data processing. The MLTable object can be used with your tabular data (for example, a CSV file containing customer churn data). MLTable is a feature of Azure Machine Learning that allows you to define and save a series of data loading steps for tabular data. This makes it easier to reproduce data loading in different environments and share it with team members. MLTable supports various data sources, including CSV and Parquet files. Figure 2-8 shows selecting AutoML in the Designer.

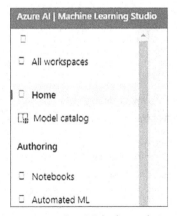

FIGURE 2-8 AutoML in the workspace

Here's how you can use MLTable with AutoML for tabular data:

1. Define Data Loading Steps: Use the mltable Python SDK (to clarify, mltable must be used via Python and not the UI) to define the steps for loading and preprocessing your data. This includes specifying the data source, filtering rows, selecting columns, and creating new columns based on the data.

2. Save Data Loading Steps: Once you have defined the data loading steps, you can save them into an MLTable file. This file contains the serialized steps, making it easy to reproduce the data loading process.

3. Load Data into a Pandas DataFrame: You can load the data defined by an MLTable into a Pandas DataFrame. This is useful for exploring the data and performing additional preprocessing before training a model.

4. Use MLTable with AutoML: When setting up an AutoML experiment for tabular data, you can use an MLTable as the data input. AutoML will automatically apply the data loading steps defined in the MLTable and use the resulting DataFrame for model training.

5. Create a Data Asset: To share the MLTable with team members and ensure reproducibility, you can create a data asset in Azure Machine Learning. This stores the MLTable in cloud storage and makes it accessible through a friendly name and version number.

6. Use Data Asset in Jobs: You can reference the data asset in Azure Machine Learning jobs, such as training or inference jobs. This allows you to use the same data loading steps consistently across different experiments and pipelines.

Here's an example of how to turn a CSV file into an MLTable using the SDK:

```
import mltable
# Define the data source (CSV file)
paths = [{'file': 'path/to/your/data.csv'}]
# Create an MLTable from the CSV file
tbl = mltable.from_delimited_files(paths)
# Apply any additional data loading steps (e.g., filtering, column selection)
tbl = tbl.filter("col('some_column') > 0")
tbl = tbl.select_columns(["column1", "column2"])
# Save the data loading steps into an MLTable file
tbl.save("./your_mltable_directory")
```

In this example, the CSV file is turned into an MLTable with some filtering and column selection steps. The resulting MLTable can then be used with AutoML for training machine learning models on tabular data.

Now that we understand how to work with tabular data in a pipeline, we can look at some specific scenarios for using AutoML on tabular data for a customer churn prediction pipeline. You can also use the Designer with AutoML and tabular data. Figure 2-9 shows creating a new AutoML run in the Designer.

FIGURE 2-9 Advanced Features of Automated Machine Learning for model development

Select and understand training options, including preprocessing and algorithms

Automated Machine Learning (AutoML) in Azure Machine Learning is a powerful tool that automates the process of selecting the best machine learning algorithms and hyperparameters for your data. This simplifies the machine learning workflow, making it accessible to data scientists, analysts, and developers, regardless of their expertise in machine learning. In the following section, we will look at automating machine learning concepts including training data, validation, featurization, preprocessing, distributed training, model selection, and ensemble learning in the context of Azure's AutoML capabilities.

- **Automated Machine Learning** AutoML in Azure provides various training options to cater to different requirements and preferences. These options are designed to optimize the model development process, ensuring efficiency and effectiveness in training machine learning models.

- **Training Data and Validation** AutoML allows users to provide training data in different formats, including MLTable for tabular data. Users can specify separate datasets for training and validation or let AutoML automatically split the training data for validation purposes. This helps in evaluating the model's performance and avoiding overfitting. For time-series forecasting, AutoML supports advanced configurations like rolling-origin cross-validation to ensure robust model evaluation.

- **Featurization and Preprocessing** AutoML automates the featurization and preprocessing steps, which are crucial for preparing the data for model training. This includes handling missing values, encoding categorical variables, and scaling numerical features. Users can customize these steps by specifying featurization settings, such as blocking certain transformers or defining custom transformations. This flexibility allows users to tailor the data preprocessing to their specific needs, ensuring that the input data is in the optimal format for training.

- **Distributed Training** For large datasets and complex models, AutoML supports distributed training. This allows the training process to be distributed across multiple compute nodes, significantly reducing the training time. Users can specify the number of nodes to use for training, enabling parallel execution of model training. Distributed training is particularly beneficial for tasks like deep learning and NLP, where the computational requirements are high.

- **Model Selection and Hyperparameter Tuning** AutoML automates the selection of machine learning algorithms and the tuning of hyperparameters. It iterates through a predefined list of algorithms and tests different hyperparameter combinations to find the best-performing model. Users can control the number of iterations and set limits on the training time to manage computational resources effectively.

- **Ensemble Models** AutoML supports ensemble models, which combine predictions from multiple models to improve accuracy. It uses techniques like voting and stacking to create ensembles, automatically selecting the best models to include in the ensemble based on their performance.

Table 2-1 outlines the algorithms that are supported by Automated Machine Learning (AutoML) in Azure Machine Learning for various learning tasks.

TABLE 2-1 Automated Machine Learning algorithms

Task Type	Algorithms
Classification	- Logistic Regression* - Light GBM* - Gradient Boosting* - Decision Tree* - K Nearest Neighbors* - Linear SVC* - Support Vector Classification (SVC) - Random Forest - Extremely Randomized Trees* - Xgboost* - Naive Bayes* - Stochastic Gradient Descent (SGD)*
Regression	- Elastic Net* - Light GBM* - Gradient Boosting* - Decision Tree* - K Nearest Neighbors* - LARS Lasso* - Stochastic Gradient Descent (SGD) - Random Forest - Extremely Randomized Trees - Xgboost* - Xgboost
Time Series Forecasting	- AutoARIMA - Prophet - Elastic Net - Light GBM - K Nearest Neighbors - Decision Tree - LARS Lasso - Extremely Randomized Trees* - Random Forest - TCNForecaster - Gradient Boosting - ExponentialSmoothing - SeasonalNaive - Average - Naive - SeasonalAverage
Image Classification	- MobileNet - ResNet - ResNeSt - SE-ResNeXt50 - ViT
Image Classification Multi-label	Refer to ClassificationMultilabelPrimaryMetrics Enum
Image Object Detection	- YOLOv5 - Faster RCNN ResNet FPN - RetinaNet ResNet FPN
NLP Text Classification Multi-label	Refer to supported algorithms for NLP tasks
NLP Text Named Entity Recognition (NER)	Refer to supported algorithms for NLP tasks

Algorithms marked with an asterisk (*) are default models.

For NLP tasks, AutoML supports a range of pretrained text DNN models, including but not limited to BERT, GPT-4, RoBERTa, T5, and LaMDA.

NEED MORE REVIEW?   **OFFICIAL ALGORITHM LIST**

If you'd like to read further about what algorithms are supported by AutoML, the list is maintained at *https://learn.microsoft.com/en-us/azure/machine-learning/ how-to-configure-auto-train?view=azureml-api-2&tabs=python#supported-algorithms*

Before showing an example of how you can select and use various training options in Automated Machine Learning (AutoML) with the Azure Machine Learning Python SDK v2, we need to list some of the options that are available:

- **Primary Metric**   This is the metric that AutoML will optimize for model selection. Common metrics include accuracy for classification tasks and mean_squared_error for regression tasks.

- **Validation Strategy**   AutoML supports several validation strategies such as cross-validation and train-validation splits. This helps in evaluating the model's performance on unseen data.

- **Max Trials**   This specifies the maximum number of different algorithm and parameter combinations that AutoML will try before selecting the best model.

- **Max Concurrent Trials**   This is the maximum number of trials that can run in parallel, which can speed up the training process.

- **Timeout**   You can set a maximum amount of time for the AutoML experiment. Once the time limit is reached, AutoML will stop trying new models.

- **Featurization**   AutoML can automatically preprocess and featurize the input data, which includes handling missing values, encoding categorical variables, and more.

The following code example shows how to configure these training options in AutoML using the Azure Machine Learning Python SDK:

```
from azure.ai.ml import MLClient
from azure.ai.ml.constants import AssetTypes
from azure.ai.ml import automl, Input
from azure.identity import DefaultAzureCredential

# Set up the MLClient
credential = DefaultAzureCredential()
subscription_id = "your-subscription-id"
resource_group = "your-resource-group"
workspace_name = "your-workspace-name"
ml_client = MLClient(credential, subscription_id, resource_group, workspace_name)

# Define the training data
training_data_input = Input(type=AssetTypes.MLTABLE, path="./data/training_data/")

# Configure the AutoML job
automl_job = automl.classification(
compute="your-compute-cluster",
experiment_name="automl_classification_example",
```

```
training_data=training_data_input,
target_column_name="target",
primary_metric="accuracy",
validation_data_split=0.2,
max_trials=100,
max_concurrent_trials=4,
timeout_minutes=60,
enable_model_explainability=True
)

# Submit the AutoML job
submitted_job = ml_client.jobs.create_or_update(automl_job)
print(f"Submitted job: {submitted_job}")

# Get the URL to monitor the job
print(f"Monitor your job at: {submitted_job.services['Studio'].endpoint}")
```

In this example, we've configured the primary metric as accuracy, set a validation data split of 20%, limited the maximum number of trials to 100, allowed up to 4 trials to run concurrently, and set a timeout of 60 minutes. We've also enabled model explainability to interpret the model's predictions.

You can adjust these options based on your specific requirements and the nature of your dataset. Whether you're a seasoned data scientist or a developer new to machine learning, AutoML provides the tools you need to develop and deploy machine learning models with ease. In the next section, we will look at the last piece of the above example: evaluating an Automated Machine Learning Run according to responsible AI guidelines.

Evaluate an automated machine learning run, including responsible AI guidelines

Depending on the type of machine learning task (classification, regression, etc.), different metrics are used to evaluate the model's performance.

Classification metrics

Classification metrics include accuracy, precision, and recall having specific meaning as ratios of true and false positives to actual positive predictions as well as metrics like F1 Score and AUC-ROC, or area under the receiver-operating curve. Monitoring the performance of your classification models using accuracy, F1 Score, or AUC-ROC to detect model drift and to decide when to retrain the model are concepts we will explore in later chapters, so it is important to understand the definitions for the following classification metrics:

- **Accuracy** Proportion of correct predictions
- **Precision** Ratio of true positives to all positive predictions
- **Recall** Ratio of true positives to all actual positives
- **F1 Score** Harmonic mean of precision and recall
- **AUC-ROC** Area under the Receiver Operating Characteristic curve

Regression Metrics

Not all supervised machine learning problems are classification problems. Regression problems could involve predicting a continuous response variable—for example, forecasting demand for a new product line requires its own set of performance metrics to measure the error between predicted and actual values. Here are a few important regression metrics that you could encounter frequently in the real world as well as on exam questions:

- **Mean Absolute Error (MAE)** Average of absolute differences between predicted and actual values
- **Mean Squared Error (MSE)** Average of squared differences between predicted and actual values
- **Root Mean Squared Error (RMSE)** Square root of MSE
- **R-squared** Proportion of variance in the dependent variable that is predictable from the independent variables

Using evaluation metrics in AutoML

When you run an AutoML experiment, it automatically calculates and logs these metrics for each model. You can access these metrics through the Azure Machine Learning Studio or programmatically using the SDK.

Visualizations for model evaluation

AutoML provides various visualizations to help you understand the model's performance:

- **Confusion Matrix** For classification tasks, this shows the number of correct and incorrect predictions for each class.
- **ROC Curve** For binary classification, this plots the true positive rate against the false positive rate at various threshold levels.
- **Precision-Recall Curve** For binary classification, this shows the trade-off between precision and recall for different threshold levels.
- **Residuals Plot** For regression tasks, this shows the difference between actual and predicted values.

After the AutoML run is complete, you can retrieve the best model based on the primary metric you specified. You can then evaluate this model on a test dataset to get a sense of its real-world performance.

Here's an example of how you can retrieve and evaluate the best model from an AutoML run:

```
from azure.ai.ml import MLClient
from azure.ai.ml.constants import AssetTypes
from azure.ai.ml import automl, Input
from azure.identity import DefaultAzureCredential

# Set up the MLClient
credential = DefaultAzureCredential()
```

```
subscription_id = "your-subscription-id"
resource_group = "your-resource-group"
workspace_name = "your-workspace-name"
ml_client = MLClient(credential, subscription_id, resource_group, workspace_name)

# Get the best model from the AutoML run
best_model = ml_client.jobs.get_best_model(
experiment_name="automl_classification_example",
job_name="automl_job_name"
)

# Evaluate the best model on a test dataset
test_data = Input(type=AssetTypes.MLTABLE, path="./data/test_data/")
evaluation_results = ml_client.jobs.evaluate(
model=best_model,
test_data=test_data
)
```

In this example, we retrieve the best model from a completed AutoML run and evaluate it on a separate test dataset. The evaluation results provide metrics that help us understand the model's performance.

> **NEED MORE REVIEW?** **AUTOMATING AND EVALUATING AUTOMATED MACHINE LEARNING RUNS**
>
> You can read further about automating and evaluating machine learning runs at *https:// learn.microsoft.com/en-us/azure/machine-learning/how-to-understand-automated-ml*

Predicting customer churn with Azure AutoML

Suppose you are a data scientist tasked with creating a machine learning model to predict customer churn for a telecom company. To accomplish this, you decide to leverage Azure's Automated Machine Learning (AutoML) feature, which simplifies the process of building and deploying models. Here's a step-by-step guide to help you prepare tabular data for use with Automated Machine Learning capabilities (see Figure 2-10 for an example using the Designer):

1. Set Up Your Environment: Create an Azure Machine Learning workspace. This is your centralized environment for managing and monitoring your machine learning models.

2. Install the Azure Machine Learning SDK v2 for Python: Run pip install azure-ai-ml in your terminal. This SDK enables you to interact with Azure Machine Learning services and resources programmatically.

3. Prepare Your Tabular Data: Gather your dataset. Ensure that your dataset includes various customer attributes and a churn label indicating whether the customer has churned.

4. Format Your Data: Structure your data in a tabular format with rows representing individual customers and columns representing attributes. The target column should be the churn label.

5. Upload Your Dataset to Azure: Convert your dataset to an MLTable and upload it to Azure. MLTable is a tabular data format supported by Azure AutoML.

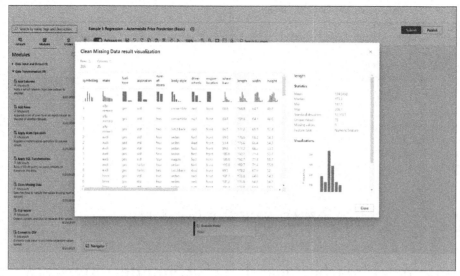

FIGURE 2-10 Data connection and feature preparation in Azure Machine Learning

Specify the task type as classification since you're predicting a binary outcome (churn or no churn). Choose accuracy as your primary metric to evaluate model performance. Also, decide on your data splitting strategy (e.g., cross-validation or train-validation split). Determine the maximum duration for the experiment (timeout minutes) and the maximum number of trials (max trials). This helps in managing computational resources and experiment time.

Run your AutoML experiment

The following code shows how to use the Azure Machine Learning SDK to submit your AutoML experiment for execution. The purpose of the code is to show in detail how to use AutoML, including configuring limits like time outs and max trials. Keep an eye on the experiment's progress through the Azure Machine Learning Studio or SDK. You can review the performance of different models as they are generated.

```
from azure.identity import DefaultAzureCredential
from azure.ai.ml import MLClient, automl, Input
from azure.ai.ml.constants import AssetTypes

# Set up workspace
credential = DefaultAzureCredential()
subscription_id = "<SUBSCRIPTION_ID>"
resource_group = "<RESOURCE_GROUP>"
workspace = "<WORKSPACE_NAME>"
ml_client = MLClient(credential, subscription_id, resource_group, workspace)

# Prepare data
train_data_input = Input(type=AssetTypes.MLTABLE, path="./data/customer_churn_data")

# Configure AutoML experiment
```

```
classification_job = automl.classification(
compute="<COMPUTE_NAME>",
experiment_name="customer_churn_prediction",
training_data=train_data_input,
 target_column_name="Churn",
primary_metric="accuracy",
n_cross_validations=5
)

# Set limits (optional)
classification_job.set_limits(
 timeout_minutes=60,
max_trials=20
)

# Run the experiment
returned_job = ml_client.jobs.create_or_update(classification_job)
print(f"Created job: {returned_job}")
```

Use automated machine learning for computer vision

Imagine you are a data scientist tasked with developing a model to classify animal images. Your goal is to utilize Azure Automated Machine Learning (AutoML) for computer vision tasks to accomplish this.

Setting up the environment

To kickstart your machine learning journey, the first step is to establish an Azure Machine Learning workspace, acting as a centralized hub for overseeing and tracking your machine learning models' progress. This workspace provides a unified platform for managing resources, conducting experiments, and deploying models seamlessly. Following this, installing the Azure Machine Learning CLI v2 and Python SDK v2 equips you with the necessary tools to interact with Azure services efficiently. These resources empower you to leverage Azure's capabilities effectively, enabling streamlined development, deployment, and management of machine learning solutions within your workspace.

Selecting the task type

In this project, the task type selected is image classification, which serves as a cornerstone determining the approach and algorithms utilized by AutoML for model training. Image classification involves categorizing images into predefined classes or categories based on their visual features. This choice significantly influences the techniques employed during the training phase, as well as the algorithms leveraged to optimize model performance.

Image classification tasks typically require specialized algorithms capable of understanding and extracting meaningful features from images to accurately classify them. AutoML, being an automated machine learning platform, adapts its approach based on the specified task type. For image classification, it employs algorithms specifically designed to process image data efficiently, such as convolutional neural networks (CNNs). CNNs are particularly well-suited for image-related tasks due to their ability to automatically learn hierarchical representations of visual features from the input images.

Furthermore, the choice of image classification as the task type underscores the importance of selecting appropriate evaluation metrics and validation strategies tailored to this specific problem domain. Metrics such as accuracy, precision, recall, and F1-score are commonly used to assess the performance of image classification models. Additionally, techniques like cross-validation or stratified sampling may be employed to ensure robust evaluation and prevent overfitting. Therefore, the decision to focus on image classification guides the entire workflow of model training within the AutoML framework, shaping the selection of algorithms, evaluation metrics, and validation strategies to achieve optimal results.

Preparing the data

Your next step is to organize your labeled image data. Format this data into JSONL format, ensuring that each line contains an image URL and the corresponding label. If your data is in a different format, such as Pascal VOC or COCO, convert it to JSONL using available helper scripts. A minimum of 10 images is recommended to start the training process. Here is an example of JSONL format to help visualize what this looks like for an image URL and a label that can have values "cat", "dog", "bird", "car", and "tree":

```
{"image_url": "http://example.com/image1.jpg", "label": "cat"}
{"image_url": "http://example.com/image2.jpg", "label": "dog"}
{"image_url": "http://example.com/image3.jpg", "label": "bird"}
{"image_url": "http://example.com/image4.jpg", "label": "car"}
{"image_url": "http://example.com/image5.jpg", "label": "tree"}
```

Create an MLTable for your training and validation data using Azure CLI or Python SDK. This involves specifying the path to your JSONL files and defining any necessary data transformations. MLTable serves as a structured representation of your data for AutoML.

Setting up compute for training

Choose a GPU-enabled compute target, such as the NC or ND series VMs, to train your computer vision models. The choice of compute target affects the speed and efficiency of model training.

Configure your AutoML experiment by setting parameters like the task type, primary metric, and job limits (e.g., `timeout_minutes`, `max_trials`, and `max_concurrent_trials`). This step involves defining the boundaries and objectives of the model training process. Figure 2-11 shows the menu for submitting an Automated ML Job including basic settings and Task settings like task type mentioned previously.

Evaluating and deploying the model

After training, evaluate the best model based on the primary metric in accordance with the responsible AI guidelines covered earlier. Register this model in your Azure Machine Learning workspace and deploy it as a web service for making predictions. This final step makes your model accessible for real-world applications. Figure 2-12 shows selecting computer vision task-specific options in AutoML and the different options available as well as where to select data for training.

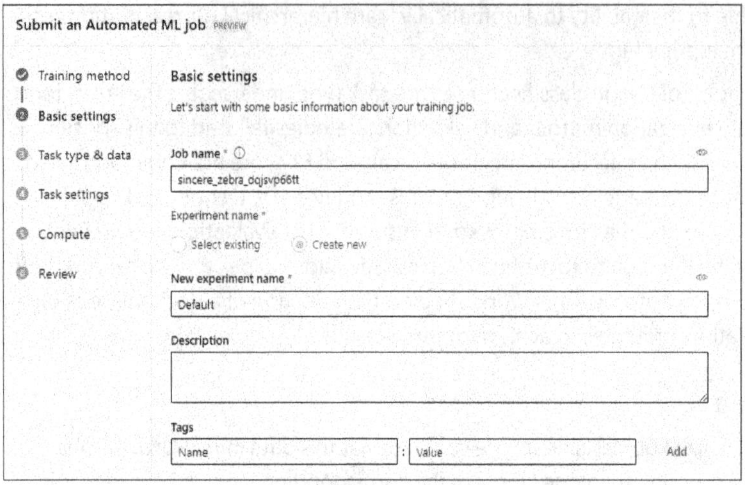

FIGURE 2-11 Submitting an AutoML job in Azure Machine Learning

> **NEED MORE REVIEW? COMPUTER VISION USING AUTOML**
>
> If you'd like to read further about compute vision using AutoML, the documentation is maintained at *https://learn.microsoft.com/en-us/azure/machine-learning/how-to-auto-train-image-models*

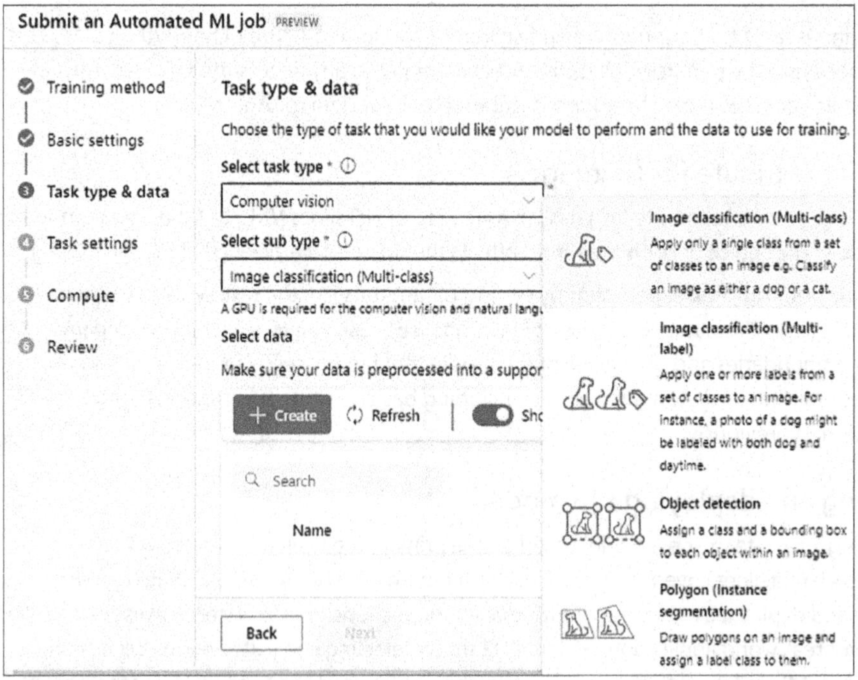

FIGURE 2-12 Select a computer vision task type using AutoML

Use automated machine learning for natural language processing (NLP)

Imagine again that you are a data scientist aiming to develop a natural language processing (NLP) model for classifying movie reviews into genres. You plan to use Azure Automated Machine Learning (AutoML) for NLP tasks. Figure 2-13 shows the high-level architecture for configuring AutoML to perform NLP tasks in Azure Machine Learning; however, in this chapter, we'll concentrate specifically on Automated Machine Learning for NLP tasks.

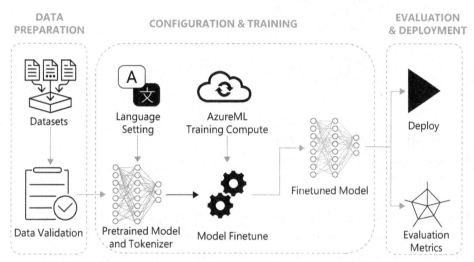

FIGURE 2-13   NLP using AutoML

Setting up the environment

The first step is to create an Azure Machine Learning workspace, which acts as a centralized platform for managing and overseeing NLP models. Additionally, configuring a GPU training compute within the workspace enhances the efficiency of training large-scale NLP models by harnessing the parallel processing power of GPUs. Moreover, installing the Azure Machine Learning CLI v2 and Python SDK v2 equips you with essential tools to seamlessly interact with Azure services. This facilitates smooth integration of NLP pipelines, experimentation, and deployment processes within your workspace. Collectively, these resources empower you to leverage Azure's capabilities effectively for developing, fine-tuning, and deploying NLP solutions with optimal performance and scalability.

Selecting the NLP task

For this project, choose `text_classification` as your NLP task. This task involves classifying each movie review into a specific genre. Organize your dataset in a CSV format with columns for the review text and the corresponding genre labels. Ensure that the data is labeled correctly for the classification task. Figure 2-14 shows how to configure an AutoML experiment for an NLP task.

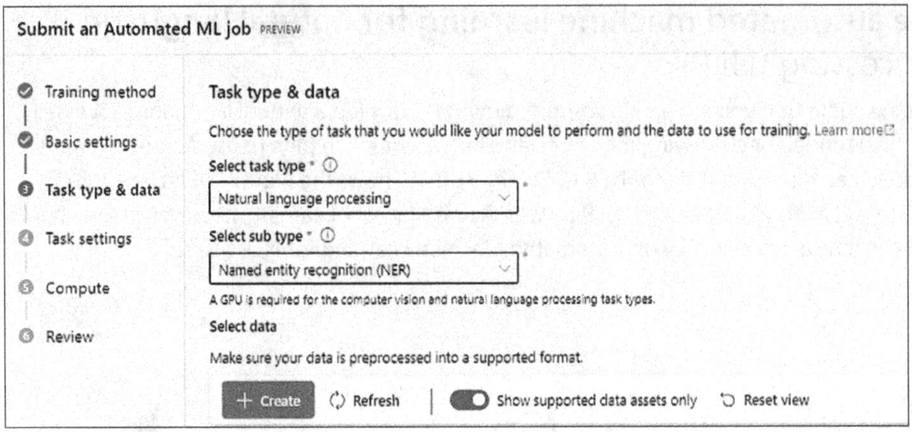

FIGURE 2-14 NLP processing task

Configuring the AutoML experiment

Define your experiment settings, including the task type (`text_classification`), compute target, and data inputs. Set the label column name to the name of the genre label column in your dataset.

Submit your AutoML job for training using the Azure CLI or Python SDK. Monitor the progress of the job and review the generated models in Azure Machine Learning Studio.

After training, evaluate the best model based on its performance metrics. Register this model in your Azure Machine Learning workspace and deploy it as a web service for making predictions. The following code example shows how to submit an AutoML NLP job:

```
from azure.ai.ml import MLClient
from azure.ai.ml.entities import AutoMLJob, TextClassificationJob, ComputeConfiguration

# Define the NLP task and settings
nlp_task = TextClassificationJob(
compute=ComputeConfiguration(target="gpu-cluster"),
training_data="path/to/training_data.csv",
validation_data="path/to/validation_data.csv",
 target_column_name="genre"
)

# Submit the AutoML job
automl_job = AutoMLJob(task=nlp_task)
ml_client.jobs.create_or_update(automl_job)
```

> **NEED MORE REVIEW?** **NLP AND AUTOML**
>
> If you'd like to read more about using AutoML to solve NLP problems in Azure Machine Learning, the documentation is maintained at *https://learn.microsoft.com/en-us/azure/machine-learning/how-to-auto-train-nlp-models*

We can also use Azure ML for fine-tuning natural language processing tasks. Figure 2-15 shows an example of fine-tuning a large language model (LLM).

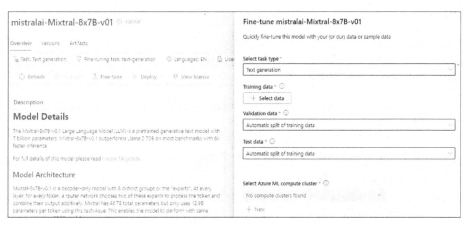

FIGURE 2-15 Fine-tuning a large language model (LLM) in Azure Machine Learning Designer

Skill 2.4: Use notebooks for custom model training

Jupyter notebooks provide an interactive environment for data science and machine learning projects. They allow you to combine executable code, rich text, visualizations, and equations in a single document. In Azure Machine Learning, Jupyter notebooks are used to develop, document, and execute code for various tasks such as data exploration, model training, and evaluation.

This skill covers how to:

- Develop code by using a compute instance
- Track model training by using MLflow
- Evaluate a model
- Train a model by using Python SDKv2
- Use the terminal to configure a compute instance

Develop code by using a compute instance

Follow these steps to set up a Jupyter notebook and attach it to a compute instance.

1. Create a Compute Instance: In your Azure Machine Learning workspace, create a new compute instance. This instance comes with Jupyter Notebook pre-installed.

2. Open Jupyter Notebook: Once the compute instance is ready, open Jupyter Notebook from the Azure ML Studio (see Figure 2-16).

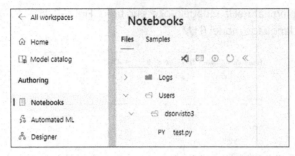

FIGURE 2-16 Opening a Jupyter notebook in Azure ML Studio

Configuring the environment in Jupyter Notebook

The first consideration is your environment. You can install additional packages using the `!pip install` command in a notebook cell. It's a good practice to list all required packages at the beginning of your notebook as follows:

```
!pip install numpy pandas scikit-learn matplotlib
```

As mentioned, another option is to use an environment. Azure Machine Learning allows you to create and use custom environments. You can specify your environment in a notebook by using the Azure ML SDK:

```
from azure.ai.ml import MLClient
from azure.ai.ml.entities import Environment

ml_client = MLClient.from_config()
my_env = Environment(
name='my-custom-env',
 conda_file='path/to/your/environment.yml'
)

ml_client.environments.create_or_update(my_env)
```

Attaching compute resources to a notebook for model training

In Azure Machine Learning, you can attach a compute instance to your Jupyter notebook for running training jobs. This provides scalable compute resources separate from your local machine. The following code shows how to connect to your Azure ML workspace, create or attach an existing compute instance like a virtual machine, and configure it for model training.

```
from azure.ai.ml import MLClient
from azure.identity import DefaultAzureCredential

# Connect to your Azure ML workspace
credential = DefaultAzureCredential()
ml_client = MLClient.from_config(credential)

# Create or attach an existing compute instance
compute_name = "my-compute-instance"
if compute_name not in ml_client.compute.list():
```

```
    # Define compute configuration
    compute_config = AmlCompute.provisioning_configuration(vm_size="STANDARD_D2_V2",
max_nodes=4)
      compute = ComputeTarget.create(ml_client.workspace, compute_name, compute_config)
    compute.wait_for_completion(show_output=True)
else:

      compute = ml_client.compute.get(compute_name)
```

Preparing data for training in a notebook

Before training your model, you must load and preprocess your data. This typically involves cleaning the data, feature engineering, and splitting it into training and test sets. The following code uses Pandas to split data into a training and test set and then scales the features to show a simple example of preparing data for model training.

```
import pandas as pd
from sklearn.model_selection import train_test_split
from sklearn.preprocessing import StandardScaler

# Load data
df = pd.read_csv('path/to/your/data.csv')

# Preprocess data

df.dropna(inplace=True)
df = pd.get_dummies(df, drop_first=True)
# Split data into features and target
X = df.drop('target_column', axis=1)
y = df['target_column']

# Split data into training and test sets
X_train, X_test, y_train, y_test = train_test_split(X, y, test_size=0.2,
random_state=42)

# Scale features
scaler = StandardScaler()
X_train = scaler.fit_transform(X_train)
X_test = scaler.transform(X_test)
```

After preparing your data, you can define and train your machine learning model. In this example, we'll use a `RandomForestClassifier` from scikit-learn:

```
from sklearn.ensemble import RandomForestClassifier
from sklearn.metrics import accuracy_score

# Define the model
model = RandomForestClassifier(n_estimators=100, random_state=42)

# Train the model
model.fit(X_train, y_train)
```

In this example, we've shown how to attach a compute instance, prepare data, and train a model in a Jupyter notebook within Azure Machine Learning. This setup allows you to leverage cloud compute resources for training more complex models on larger datasets. This was a very simple example; in the final section of this chapter, we will provide a more realistic model training scenario.

Track model training by using MLflow

Data scientists harness the power of notebooks as indispensable tools for model experimentation and training. To effectively manage the plethora of model training outcomes, organizing them into experiments becomes imperative. MLflow emerges as a key facilitator in this process, offering robust logging capabilities to track model metrics seamlessly within notebook environments. What is MLflow? MLflow is an open-source framework for tracking experiments and storing artifacts like models. It has a powerful tool called a model registry that allows you not only to track metrics, parameters, and models that are part of your experiments but also to query the registry and share models for deployment once they meet the requirements of your solution.

Creating an MLflow experiment is the initial step toward structured model management. By grouping runs within experiments, data scientists gain clarity and organization in their workflow. MLflow simplifies this task by allowing the creation of custom experiments tailored to specific projects, ensuring that model training outcomes are neatly categorized for analysis.

Upon setting up the experiment, logging results with MLflow becomes the next focus. Here, data scientists can utilize autologging or opt for custom logging based on project requirements. Autologging, a feature supported by MLflow, automates the tracking of metrics, parameters, artifacts, and models for popular machine learning libraries. This streamlines the logging process, providing efficiency and consistency across model runs. Alternatively, custom logging offers greater flexibility, enabling data scientists to manually log supplementary or custom information as needed. Once the model training is complete, data scientists can easily review all logged metrics within the MLflow environment, facilitating analysis and decision-making. The following code snippet shows how to perform autologging with MLflow in a notebook, and Figure 2-17 shows the output.

```
from xgboost import XGBClassifier
with mlflow.start_run():
    mlflow.xgboost.autolog()
    model = XGBClassifier(use_label_encoder=False, eval_metric="logloss")
    model.fit(X_train, y_train, eval_set=[(X_test, y_test)], verbose=False)
```

> ***NEED MORE REVIEW?*** **TRACKING MODELS FOR TRAINING USING MLFLOW AND NOTEBOOKS**
>
> You can read more about tracking models using MLflow in a Jupyter notebook here: *https://learn.microsoft.com/en-us/training/modules/track-model-training-jupyter-notebooks-mlflow/*

Custom logging with MLflow provides data scientists with the flexibility to manually log supplementary or custom information that may not be captured through autologging. This feature allows for finer control over the logging process, enabling data scientists to tailor their logging efforts to specific project requirements. By utilizing common functions such as `mlflow.log_param`, `mlflow.log_metric`, `mlflow.log_artifact`, and `mlflow.log_model`, data scientists can capture key parameters, metrics, files, and models, respectively, enhancing the depth of analysis and insight into model performance.

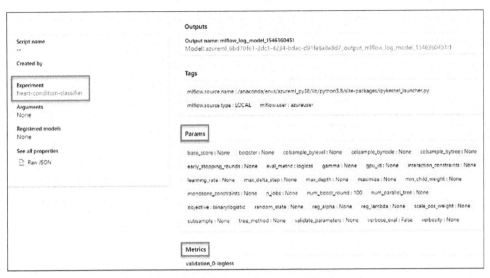

FIGURE 2-17 Tracking model training in MLflow from a Jupyter notebook

Evaluate a model

We can evaluate models generated by automated machine learning experiments. You can employ a comprehensive approach encompassing various metrics and visualizations. Initially, after completing an experiment, accessing job results via Azure Machine Learning Studio or Jupyter notebooks is crucial. Once obtained, a plethora of classification metrics aids in dissecting model performance, including accuracy, precision, recall, and area under the ROC curve (AUC). These metrics offer insights into different facets of classification effectiveness, facilitating informed decision-making regarding model selection. Additionally, visual aids such as confusion matrices provide intuitive representations of classification errors, while ROC and precision-recall curves illustrate the model's discriminatory power across different thresholds. Further insights can be gleaned from cumulative gains, lift, and calibration curves, which respectively showcase the model's ability to identify positive samples, its performance relative to random guessing, and its calibration of prediction confidence. Table 2-2 shows some common metrics for evaluating a model. Figure 2-18 shows an ROC curve for a model.

TABLE 2-2 Evaluating a model

Metric	Description
AUC	Area under the ROC curve
Accuracy	Ratio of predictions matching true labels
Avg. Precision	Weighted mean of precisions at each recall increase

Metric	Description
Balanced Accuracy	Mean recall for each class
F1 Score	Harmonic mean of precision and recall
Log Loss	Negative log-likelihood of true labels given predictions
Matthews Correlation	Balanced accuracy measure
Precision	Avoiding labeling negative samples as positive
Recall	Detecting all positive samples
Weighted Accuracy	Accuracy weighted by class samples

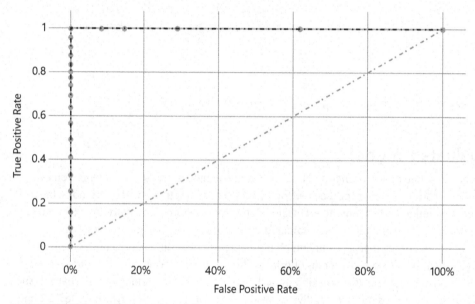

FIGURE 2-18 ROC curve for a good model

Train a model by using Python SDKv2

Training a model using the Python SDKv2 is similar, but there are some differences compared to using a notebook. A major difference is with job submission. Job submission is required rather than executing code cells interactively within a notebook. You submit a training job to the Azure Machine Learning service. This job orchestrates the execution of the training script on the configured compute resources. By submitting a job, you can track the progress of the training process, monitor resource utilization, and leverage features like distributed training for improved efficiency and scalability. By understanding confidence levels, you can assess the model's ability to correctly assign confidence to its predictions. Follow these high-level steps to train a model using the Python SDKv2:

1. Workspace Setup: Instead of directly working within a notebook, you first establish a connection to your Azure Machine Learning workspace. This centralized workspace provides a structured environment for managing all your machine learning resources, including datasets, models, and experiments. Unlike a notebook, where resources are often scattered, the workspace ensures organization and collaboration across projects.

2. Script Development: Rather than writing all your code directly in a notebook, you create a separate Python script (`main.py`) specifically for training the model. This script contains functions for data preprocessing, model training, and evaluation. By separating code into a script, you can maintain a clean and modular structure, facilitating easier testing, debugging, and version control compared to working within a notebook.

3. Compute Configuration: Instead of relying solely on the compute instance provided by the notebook environment, you configure specific compute resources for running the training job. This allows you to choose the appropriate compute instance or cluster based on the workload requirements, such as CPU or GPU resources, memory, and scalability. By configuring dedicated compute resources, you ensure optimal performance and resource utilization for training large-scale models.

Use the terminal to configure a compute instance

When working in Azure Machine Learning, sometimes you need more than just notebooks to get things done. That's when accessing the terminal of a compute instance comes in handy. It's like having a command prompt or terminal window right within your workspace.

With access to the terminal, you can do a few things:

- **Use files from Git and version files** This means you can work with files stored in your workspace's file system, and you're not limited to just one compute instance. So, if you have code or data in Git repositories, you can access and work with them directly from the terminal.

- **Install packages** Sometimes, you might need additional libraries or packages for your work. With terminal access, you can easily install these packages on the compute instance you're using.

- **Create extra kernels** Kernels are like environments where your code runs. By creating extra kernels, you can set up different environments for running your code, which can be useful for testing or experimenting with different setups.

To access the terminal, you simply go to your workspace in Azure Machine Learning studio, navigate to the Notebooks section, and then open the terminal from there. If there's no compute instance running, you can start or create one right from the Compute section. Once you have the compute instance in a running state, you can access its attached terminal. Figure 2-19 shows how to access the terminal from Notebooks.

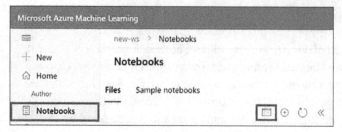

FIGURE 2-19 Accessing a terminal from Notebooks

Skill 2.5: Tune hyperparameters with Azure Machine Learning

Hyperparameter tuning is an essential step in the machine learning pipeline. It involves finding the optimal combination of hyperparameters that maximizes the performance of your model. Azure Machine Learning provides a robust framework for automating this process.

> **This skill covers how to:**
> - Select a sampling method
> - Define the primary metric
> - Define early termination options

Select a sampling method

Azure Machine Learning provides several methods for sampling the hyperparameter space, each suitable for different scenarios and requirements. This tutorial explores the three main sampling methods supported by Azure ML: Random, Grid, and Bayesian sampling.

Random sampling

Random sampling is versatile, supporting both discrete and continuous hyperparameters. It randomly selects values from a defined search space, allowing for the early termination of low-performance jobs. This method is particularly useful for an initial broad search across the search space, which can later be refined to focus on promising regions. Here's an example of random sampling with Azure ML:

```
from azure.ai.ml.sweep import Normal, Uniform, RandomParameterSampling
command_job_for_sweep = command_job(
learning_rate=Normal(mu=10, sigma=3),
keep_probability=Uniform(min_value=0.05, max_value=0.1),
batch_size=Choice(values=[16, 32, 64, 128]),
)

sweep_job = command_job_for_sweep.sweep(
```

```
compute="cpu-cluster",
  sampling_algorithm="random"
)
```

Sobol extension

Sobol, a quasi-random sequence, improves the distribution across the search space and allows for reproducibility using a seed. Here's an example of Sobol sampling:

```
from azure.ai.ml.sweep import RandomParameterSampling

sweep_job = command_job_for_sweep.sweep(
compute="cpu-cluster",
sampling_algorithm=RandomParameterSampling(seed=123, rule="sobol")
)
```

Grid sampling

Grid sampling is ideal for discrete hyperparameters when you can afford an exhaustive search. It performs a simple grid search over all possible values, also supporting the early termination of low-performance runs. Here's an example of grid sampling with Azure ML:

```
from azure.ai.ml.sweep import Choice

command_job_for_sweep = command_job(

_size=Choice(values=[16, 32]),

number_of_hidden_layers=Choice(values=[1,2,3]),

)

sweep_job = command_job_for_sweep.sweep(

compute="cpu-cluster",

sampling_algorithm="grid"
)
```

Bayesian sampling

Based on Bayesian optimization, this method selects samples based on the performance of previous samples to continuously improve the primary metric. It's recommended for scenarios with a sufficient budget to explore the hyperparameter space thoroughly. Here's an example of Bayesian sampling with Azure ML:

```
from azure.ai.ml.sweep import Uniform, Choice

command_job_for_sweep = command_job(
learning_rate=Uniform(min_value=0.05, max_value=0.1),
batch_size=Choice(values=[16, 32, 64, 128]
)

sweep_job = command_job_for_sweep.sweep(
compute="cpu-cluster",
sampling_algorithm="bayesian"    ...
)
```

Choosing the right sampling method depends on the specific needs of your project, such as the type of hyperparameters, the size of the search space, and the computational budget. Random sampling provides a broad initial search, grid sampling covers all possibilities within a limited set, and Bayesian sampling optimizes based on learning from past evaluations. Each of these methods can be implemented easily within Azure Machine Learning, providing powerful tools to enhance your model's performance. Figure 2-20 shows a metric chart visualizing this performance for an example hyperparameter.

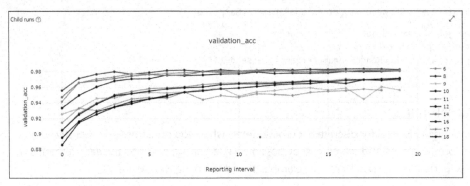

FIGURE 2-20 A metrics chart

Define the primary metric

The search space defines the range of values for each hyperparameter. You can specify discrete values using Choice or continuous ranges using Uniform or Normal distributions.

```
from azure.ai.ml.sweep import Choice, Uniform

search_space = {
 "learning_rate": Uniform(min_value=0.01, max_value=0.1),
 "batch_size": Choice(values=[16, 32, 64, 128])
}
```

I mentioned the concept of a primary metric when we discussed algorithms in AutoML. You might recall that the primary metric is the performance measure that the tuning process aims to optimize. You need to specify the metric name and whether to maximize or minimize it.

```
primary_metric = {
    "name": "accuracy",
    "goal": "Maximize"
}
```

Define early termination options

Early termination policies allow you to stop low-performing training runs early, saving time and resources. Azure Machine Learning supports several policies such as Bandit, Median StRopping, and Truncation Selection.

NEED MORE REVIEW? **HYPERPARAMETER TUNING**

If you'd like to read further about hyperparameter tuning in Azure Machine Learning, the documentation is maintained at *https://learn.microsoft.com/en-us/azure/machine-learning/how-to-tune-hyperparameters*

Chapter summary

- You can access and wrangle data during interactive development with Apache Spark, focusing on preparing and manipulating data through various assets and stores.

- You can build machine learning models for tabular data, computer vision, and natural language processing by employing custom code components in the Designer interface and adhering to responsible AI guidelines during model evaluations.

- You can leverage Automated Machine Learning to efficiently model different types of data including tabular, image, and text. This involves selecting the best training options, preprocessing, and algorithms, and ensuring responsible AI practices in model evaluation.

- You can develop and train models using custom code in Jupyter notebooks, track experiments with MLflow, and manage compute instances through the terminal to enhance the model training process.

Thought experiment

In this thought experiment, demonstrate your skills and knowledge of the topics covered in this chapter. You can find the answers in the section that follows.

1. You are tasked with exploring data using Azure Machine Learning. Which method would best utilize data assets and datastores while being user-friendly?

   A. Employing R notebooks for data analysis.

   B. Accessing data via direct database queries.

   C. Using Apache Spark for interactive data wrangling.

   D. Implementing a manual data cleanup process.

2. When creating models using the Azure Machine Learning Designer, which component is essential for handling natural language processing tasks effectively?

   A. Using a prebuilt regression model.

   B. Incorporating a custom code component.

   C. Applying a clustering algorithm.

   D. Configuring a neural network for image processing.

3. In the context of using Automated Machine Learning, how should you approach the selection of preprocessing options for a tabular data project to ensure optimal model performance?

A. Select only the default preprocessing options.

B. Customize preprocessing options based on data type.

C. Ignore preprocessing to reduce complexity.

D. Use extensive data augmentation techniques.

4. During custom model training, what is the most effective way to manage and track custom model training experiments in Jupyter notebooks?

A. Documenting changes manually in a shared document.

B. Using Python SDKv2 without additional tracking.

C. Tracking experiments with MLflow and configuring compute instances via the terminal.

D. Relying solely on automated model evaluation tools.

Thought experiment answers

This section contains the solutions to the thought experiment. Each answer explains why the answer choice is correct.

1. The answer is **C.** Using Apache Spark for interactive data wrangling effectively utilizes data assets and datastores, aligning with the focus of Skill 2.1. Option A involves using R, which is not mentioned in the chapter's focus. Option B might not interact directly with the set data assets and datastores, and Option D adds unnecessary complexity.

2. The answer is **B**. Incorporating a custom code component in the Azure Machine Learning Designer allows for effective handling of natural language processing tasks, as indicated in Skill 2.2. Options A, C, and D do not specifically address NLP and may not be as effective in this context.

3. The answer is **B**. Customizing preprocessing options based on data type ensures optimal model performance when using Automated Machine Learning for tabular data. Option A does not consider the specific needs of the data, Option C neglects a crucial part of model training, and Option D is inappropriate for tabular data and more suited to image data.

4. The answer is **C**. Tracking experiments with MLflow and managing compute instances via the terminal is the most effective way mentioned in the chapter for managing and tracking custom model training in Jupyter notebooks. Option A lacks the structure and integration with Azure services, Option B omits experiment tracking, and Option D does not provide a comprehensive solution for experiment management.

## CHAPTER 3

Prepare a model for deployment

While you read through this chapter, remember that exploring data and training models are iterative processes. With each iteration, you'll gain deeper insights into your data and refine your models for better accuracy and performance. After acquiring the three skills in this chapter, you will be able to combine them to build training pipelines using automated machine learning and tune hyperparameters to iteratively improve the model performance using Azure Machine Learning (Azure ML).

Skills covered in this chapter:

- Skill 3.1: Run model training scripts
- Skill 3.2: Implement training pipelines
- Skill 3.3: Manage models in Azure Machine Learning

Skill 3.1: Run model training scripts

When we write code, we want to minimize repetition, following DRY (don't repeat yourself) principles. But when we are learning the many features of Azure Machine Learning—with concepts like jobs, runs, training scripts, compute targets, and MLflow—repetition is beneficial for understanding how all these pieces fit together to provide capabilities that satisfy our functional and nonfunctional requirements, meeting our design objectives. For example, after this chapter you will be able to run a training script using a job and configure a compute target for that job to enable a scalable training scenario using Apache Spark pools. You will learn to design an experiment tracking solution using MLflow to log metrics and artifacts from training runs, which helps in analyzing and comparing models across multiple runs. Before exploring this, we'll cover the concepts of job runs, the distinction between jobs and runs, and the available configuration options.

This skill covers how to:

- Configure job run settings for a script
- Configure the compute for a job run
- Consume data from a data asset in a job
- Run a script as a job by using Azure Machine Learning
- Use MLflow to log metrics from a job run
- Use logs to troubleshoot job run errors
- Configure an environment for a job run
- Define parameters for a job

Configure job run settings for a script

In Azure Machine Learning, you have multiple options for creating a training job. These include utilizing the command line interface (CLI), the REST API, or the user interface (UI) directly within Azure Machine Learning Studio. Each method provides flexibility and caters to different preferences and expertise levels, ensuring that you can choose the most suitable approach for your needs.

This guide emphasizes the process of using your own data and code to train a machine learning model within Azure Machine Learning Studio. By leveraging the studio's structured environment, you can streamline your workflow and maintain organization throughout the model development process. The studio offers a user-friendly interface that simplifies the integration of data, code, and various machine learning tools.

Training a machine learning model in Azure Machine Learning Studio involves several key steps. First, you must prepare and upload your data, ensuring it is in the correct format. Next, you can create and configure your training script, specifying the algorithms and parameters required for your model. Finally, you initiate the training job through the studio, monitoring progress and evaluating results to refine your model as needed.

> **IMPORTANT CONFIGURING JOB RUN SETTINGS FOR A SCRIPT FEATURE IS IN PUBLIC PREVIEW**
>
> Configuring job run settings for a script is in public preview at the time of this writing, meaning it's not fully supported for production workloads yet and may have limited features.

There are a few prerequisites for setting this up, and we've covered most of them in previous chapters, but to recap, the prerequisites are:

- An Azure subscription. If you don't have one, you can create a free account.
- An Azure Machine Learning workspace. You can follow the instructions below to create one if you don't have one yet.
- A basic understanding of what a job is in Azure Machine Learning.

To begin managing your machine learning experiments in Azure Machine Learning Studio, first start by signing in to your account. Once logged in, choose the appropriate subscription and workspace to work within. From the home page, proceed to initiate a new job by selecting Create New and then Job to access the job creation interface, where you can configure and launch your machine learning tasks.

1. Sign in to Azure Machine Learning Studio.

2. Select your subscription and workspace.

3. Navigate to the job creation UI from the home page by selecting Create New and then Job.

At this point, you will see some basic configuration settings (see Figure 3-1) as detailed below:

- **Job Name**   This uniquely identifies your job and is also used as the display name

- **Experiment Name**   This organizes the job in the Azure Machine Learning studio, under the corresponding experiment in the studio's "Experiment" tab.

- **Existing Experiment**   By default, jobs are placed in the Default experiment.

- **Description**   Optionally, add a description for your job.

- **Timeout**   Specify the maximum number of hours the entire training job is allowed to run. The job will be canceled if this limit is reached.

- **Tags**   Add tags to your job to help with organization.

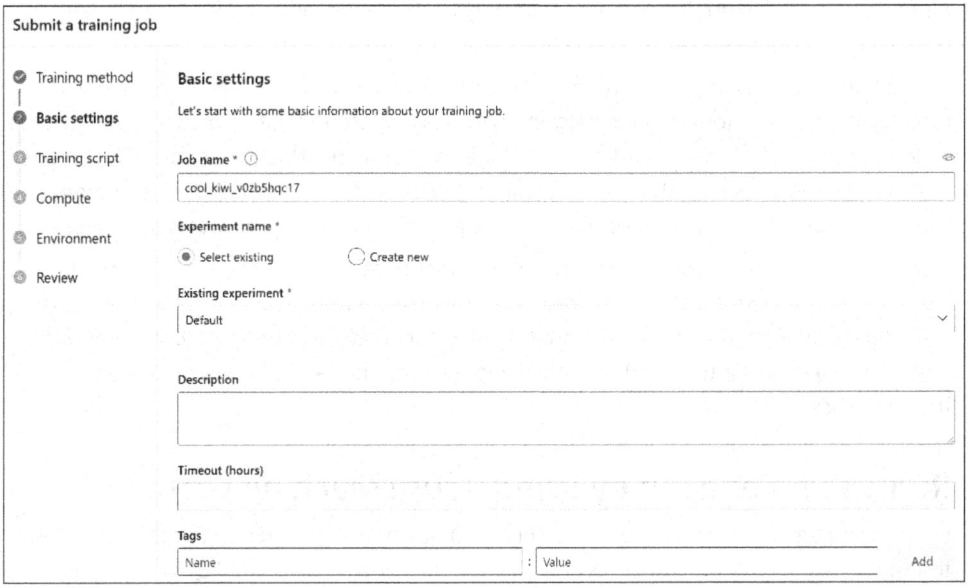

FIGURE 3-1 Job run settings for a script

Configure the compute for a job run

Selecting the right compute target is crucial for effectively training your machine learning model in Azure Machine Learning. Depending on your training needs, you can choose from various options such as CPU-based or GPU-based virtual machines (VMs). Each type offers distinct advantages: CPU-based virtual machines are generally more cost-effective for less intensive tasks, while GPU-based virtual machines provide the high processing power needed for more complex computations and deep learning tasks.

For larger-scale training jobs, Azure Machine Learning compute clusters are an excellent choice. These clusters allow for scalable, distributed computing, enabling you to handle substantial workloads efficiently. Compute clusters can automatically adjust their size based on your requirements, ensuring optimal resource usage and cost management.

Ultimately, the choice of compute target should align with the specific demands of your training process. Consider factors such as the complexity of your model, the volume of data, and your budget constraints. By carefully selecting the appropriate compute resources, you can optimize both the performance and cost-efficiency of your machine learning projects.

Consume data from a data asset in a job

Managing and versioning your training data is streamlined with Azure Machine Learning datasets. These datasets provide a structured way to organize, label, and maintain your data, ensuring consistency and traceability throughout your machine learning projects. By using Azure Machine Learning datasets, you can easily track changes and updates to your data, facilitating reproducibility and collaboration.

Accessing the data in your training script can be achieved by either mounting or downloading the dataset. Mounting the dataset allows you to read the data directly from its source without duplicating it, which is efficient for large datasets and reduces storage requirements. Alternatively, downloading the dataset copies the data locally to your compute environment, which is useful for scenarios where extensive data manipulation or preprocessing is necessary.

Choosing between mounting and downloading depends on your specific use case and workflow. Mounting is ideal for read-heavy operations and when working with large datasets, while downloading is beneficial for more intensive data manipulation tasks. Both methods ensure seamless access to your data, enhancing the efficiency and effectiveness of your model training process.

Run a script as a job by using Azure Machine Learning

Imagine you are a data scientist at a healthcare company, and your task is to develop a predictive model that can identify patients at high risk of developing diabetes. You will use patient data such as age, weight, blood pressure, and blood sugar levels for this purpose. This guide will walk you through the steps to train your model in Azure Machine Learning. We ultimately want to get to the point where we can integrate MLflow into our job and log experiment metrics.

The first step is to configure a job run as we have seen previously. The objective is to define how your training script is executed so you can do the following (for clarification, you should already have a training script that contains your model training code called train.py):

- Define any arguments or parameters that your script requires
- Specify the environment with the necessary dependencies

You can then configure a compute for your job run. You can choose between Azure ML Compute Clusters for scalable training or virtual machines for smaller workloads. Or, if you require distributed training, you might consider Spark pools as covered in earlier chapters. Next, you would consume data from a data asset, which may be physically stored in Azure Blob Storage or another supported storage service. We also need to upload our source code, which can be stored either in the workspace's default Blob Storage or on your local machine. The training script step points to this source code. When the training job starts, the command you define will execute in the context of the root directory of your source code and will execute your scripts.

To accomplish the above, you need to use the training script step for submitting a training job in Azure Machine Learning. You need to upload your source code and configure any required inputs or outputs for the job. You also need to specify the command that will execute your training script. There are also data assets that are inputs. Table 3-1 summarizes this information.

TABLE 3-1 Code, inputs, and command overview

Aspect	Description
Code	This can be a file or a folder from your local machine or from your workspace's default Blob Storage. Once you select your code, Azure will display the files to be uploaded.
Inputs	You can specify various types of inputs, such as data, integer, number, Boolean, or string.
Command	This is the command that will be executed to start the training job. You can write command-line arguments directly into the command or use curly braces notation to infer them from other sections, particularly inputs. When using an input in the command, you should specify the input name using the format `${{inputs.input_name}}`. For example, if you have an input named wiki, you can refer to it in the command as `--data ${{inputs.wiki}}`.

Since the command runs from the root directory of the uploaded code folder, if your code is in a subdirectory, you should use the relative path to refer to it in the command. For instance, if your main script main.py is located in the src subdirectory, the command would be `python ./src/main.py` followed by any other command-line arguments.

> **NEED MORE REVIEW?** **SUBMITTING A TRAINING JOB**
>
> You can read more about submitting a training job in Azure ML Studio at *https://learn.microsoft.com/en-us/azure/machine-learning/how-to-train-with-ui?view=azureml-api-2*

Use MLflow to log metrics from a job run

Imagine you're working on a machine learning project to predict customer churn. You've designed a robust training script, but you need a way to track the performance of your model over multiple runs and compare different models. This is where MLflow comes into play.

MLflow is an open-source platform that helps you manage the end-to-end machine learning lifecycle. It allows you to track experiments, package code into reproducible runs, and share and deploy models. It's particularly useful for tracking metrics during training, such as accuracy and loss, which can help you identify the best-performing models.

Why use MLflow?

There are several reasons to use MLflow, the least of which is experiment reproducibility. Reproducibility requires the design to have a mechanism to track metrics associated with experiments such as accuracy, precision, and recall for each training run. This is known as *experiment tracking*. There is an added benefit of being able to search, filter, and compare models based on these performance metrics. We might build ways to analyze experiments and determine the best model for a sequence of performance metrics. Since we are using MLflow, we have all the metrics and artifacts (models themselves) and a way to track which version of the model was associated with which data assets and the specific metrics we are interested in as part of the training run. We will look at tracking metrics, comparing models, and model versioning, and how all three of these concepts feed into the idea of reproducibility.

- **Track Metrics**   Log and visualize metrics such as accuracy, precision, and recall for each training run.
- **Compare Models**   Easily compare different models based on their performance metrics.
- **Reproducibility**   The concept of experiment reproducibility as defined in Chapter 1. Record and version your experiments to ensure reproducibility.
- **Model Versioning**   Models must be versioned because we need a way to distinguish similar models in the same experiment that have different performance metrics.

Integrate MLflow into your training script

MLflow is an open-source library, and the simplest way to integrate it into your training scripts is installing it in your script (a more advanced way to do this would be to configure an environment, but we will cover this next). You can start by importing MLflow into your training script, giving you access to all the functionality of the `mlflow` library.

Once imported, you can log metrics using `mlflow.log_metric`, specifying accuracy as the key and passing in the `accuracy_score`.

You can log metrics after each epoch or iteration. Optionally, we can log model parameters and other artifacts for more comprehensive tracking. One artifact we might want to track are data assets associated with model training for reproducibility since you might want to retrain the model in the future and understand whether data drift has occurred.

So, we can now integrate MLflow into our notebooks, but what about running MLflow as part of a job? Before we cover this, we want to ensure that we have set up MLflow's tracking URI. Figure 3-2 shows model metrics logged in MLflow.

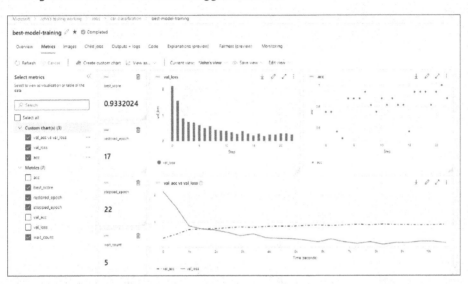

FIGURE 3-2 Model metrics logged in MLflow

Setting the MLflow tracking URI

Configure the MLflow tracking URI to point to your Azure ML workspace. This allows MLflow to store experiment data in a centralized location. Here are some tips for using the tracking URI and how to monitor progress for training runs:

- Use the Azure ML SDK to get the tracking URI: `tracking_uri = Workspace.from_config().get_mlflow_tracking_uri()`.
- Set the tracking URI in your script: `mlflow.set_tracking_uri(tracking_uri)`.
- If you decide to submit your training script as a job in Azure ML Studio, ensure that MLflow is included in your environment's dependencies.
- Monitor the progress of your training runs and view logged metrics in real time.

Logging models

As covered in the previous section, an added benefit of using MLflow is the ability to analyze and compare models. After training is complete, use MLflow's UI (the local instance on port 5000) to compare the performance of different models and select the best model based on the metrics logged during training.

You are free to define the criteria that makes a "best model" based on your use case and search the registry for the best model. Since you have set up MLflow to log metrics, all this data is available for analysis, which offers some unique applications in terms of creating dashboards and other ways to continuously monitor the performance of our models. Table 3-2 summarizes some of the options available for analysis.

TABLE 3-2 Logging methods in MLflow

Logged Value	Example Code	Notes
Log text in a text file	`mlflow.log_text("text string", "notes.txt")`	Text is persisted inside of the run in a text file with the specified name.
Log dictionaries as JSON and YAML files	`mlflow.log_dict(dictionary, "file.yaml")`	The dictionary is persisted as a JSON or YAML file with the specified filename.
Log a trivial file already existing	`mlflow.log_artifact("path/to/file.pkl")`	Files are logged in the root of the run. If an artifact path is provided, the file is logged in a folder according to it.
Log all the artifacts in an existing folder	`mlflow.log_artifacts("path/to/folder")`	Folder structure is copied to the run, excluding the root folder indicated.

> **NEED MORE REVIEW?** **MLFLOW FOR TRACKING AND LOGGING METRICS FOR JOB RUNS**
>
> If you'd like to read further about using MLflow to track and log metrics from a job run, you can read the official documentation at *https://learn.microsoft.com/en-us/azure/ machine-learning/how-to-use-mlflow-cli-runs?view=azureml-api-2#configure-the-experiment*

Use logs to troubleshoot job run errors

Effectively debugging and monitoring your Azure Machine Learning (Azure ML) workloads relies on understanding logs, traces, and metrics. These tools are essential for diagnosing issues and ensuring the smooth operation of your machine learning experiments. Let's dive into how these elements help, using a practical scenario.

Imagine you're working on a machine learning experiment in Azure ML, and you hit an unexpected error during the training phase. To figure out what went wrong, you need to check the logs that Azure ML generates. Logs are detailed records of events and errors that occur during your experiment, giving you insights into what might have caused the failure. Traces, which provide a step-by-step account of the operations, help you understand the sequence of events leading up to the error. Metrics, offering numerical data about things like resource usage and performance, can highlight potential issues like bottlenecks or inefficiencies.

Navigating through the Azure ML interface, you can find these logs, traces, and metrics for your experiment. Reviewing the logs, you'll see specific error messages and the context of the failure. Traces will show you the exact steps taken before the error occurred, making it easier to pinpoint the issue. Metrics give you a broader view of your experiment's performance, helping you spot patterns or anomalies that could be contributing to the problem. By combining these insights, you can figure out how to fix the issue and successfully rerun your experiment, improving your debugging and monitoring skills.

Identifying relevant log files

There are several log files you must be familiar with for debugging a failed run. See Table 3-3 for a list of common log files in a troubleshooting scenario.

TABLE 3-3 Summary of log files

Log File Name	Description
20_image_build_log.txt	Contains Docker build logs, helpful during environment updates. It also provides image registry details upon a successful build.
55_azureml-execution.txt	Logs the process of pulling the image to the compute target.
65_job_prep.txt	Details the job preparation process, including downloading your code and datastores to the compute target.
70_driver_log.txt	Captures standard output from your script, including print statements. This log typically contains execution-related logs from your code.

When debugging a failed run in Azure Machine Learning, familiarity with various log files is crucial. Each log file provides specific insights into different stages of the machine learning experiment, helping you identify and resolve issues efficiently. Table 3-3 summarizes the common log files you'll encounter in a troubleshooting scenario, each serving a unique purpose in the debugging process.

The 20_image_build_log.txt file contains Docker build logs, which are especially useful during environment updates. This log file provides details about the image registry once the build is successful, allowing you to verify that the environment has been set up correctly. Any issues related to Docker image creation or registry can be traced back to this log, making it an essential resource during the initial setup phase.

The 55_azureml-execution.txt and 65_job_prep.txt files focus on the execution and preparation stages, respectively. The 55_azureml-execution.txt log records the process of pulling the image to the compute target, ensuring that the necessary environment is in place before running your code. Meanwhile, the 65_job_prep.txt log details the job preparation process, including downloading your code and datastores to the compute target. This helps confirm that all necessary resources are correctly prepared and available for execution.

Finally, the 70_driver_log.txt file captures the standard output from your script, including any print statements and execution-related logs. This log is particularly valuable for understanding the behavior of your code during runtime, providing direct feedback from your script's execution. Reviewing this log can help you identify errors or unexpected behavior in your code, making it a vital tool for pinpointing the root cause of a failed run.

Accessing logs in Azure ML Studio

Understanding which log files are relevant for debugging your Azure Machine Learning (Azure ML) runs is only the first step. Knowing how to access these logs is equally important for effective troubleshooting. Azure ML provides a straightforward way to navigate and retrieve these logs, ensuring that you have the necessary information at your fingertips when diagnosing issues.

Begin by navigating to Azure ML Studio. In the studio, go to your workspace, select the experiment you are working on, and then choose the specific run you need to investigate. Within the run's details, an Outputs And Logs section contains all the log files associated with that run. This centralized location makes it easy to locate and review the logs, enabling you to quickly identify and address any problems.

Real-time monitoring is also possible by streaming logs directly to your local terminal. This feature is particularly useful for actively running experiments, as it allows you to monitor the logs as they are generated, providing immediate feedback on your experiment's progress and any potential issues. We understand which log files are relevant, but can we better understand how to access them? In order to do this, you can follow a few steps in the workspace:

1. Navigate to Azure ML Studio.

2. Go to Workspace > Experiment > Run > Outputs And Logs to find the log files for your specific experiment.

3. Stream logs: In order to stream logs in real-time to your local terminal, you need to use the Azure Machine Learning CLI or SDK. This allows you to monitor the logs as they are generated, providing immediate feedback on your experiment's progress and any potential issues.

For real-time monitoring, you can stream logs directly to your local terminal (appearing under standard out) using the following Python code:

```
from azureml.core import Workspace, Experiment, ScriptRunConfig
ws = Workspace.from_config()
config = ScriptRunConfig(...)
run = Experiment(ws, 'my-amazing-experiment').submit(config)
run.wait_for_completion(show_output=True)
```

The above pattern is standard for many applications including data science and ML applications. Figure 3-3 shows an example of an important log: the driver log.

> **NEED MORE REVIEW?** **LOGGING BEST PRACTICES**
>
> You can read more about the syslog standard and best practices in Azure here:
> *https://learn.microsoft.com/en-us/azure/azure-monitor/agents/data-sources-syslog*

FIGURE 3-3 Driver log for debugging

SSH for debugging

Sometimes, debugging your machine learning experiments requires more direct interaction with your compute instance or target. SSH (secure shell) access allows you to log in to the compute instance, providing a powerful way to diagnose and troubleshoot issues that aren't immediately apparent from logs and metrics. This direct access can be crucial for understanding the environment in which your code runs, investigating resource utilization, and making real-time adjustments.

Enabling SSH access is a step that must be taken during the creation of your compute instance. When setting up your compute target in Azure ML Studio, ensure that SSH access is enabled by specifying the appropriate settings. This preparation is essential because it allows you to access the instance later without additional reconfiguration. Having SSH access enabled from the beginning can save valuable time when a debugging issue arises, as you'll be ready to dive into the instance immediately.

Once SSH is enabled, retrieving the necessary connection details is straightforward. Navigate to the Compute tab in Azure ML Studio, where you can find the public IP address and port number for your compute target. These details are required to establish an SSH connection from your local machine. With this information, you can use any SSH client to connect to your compute instance, providing you with a command-line interface to perform in-depth diagnostics, inspect running processes, and directly interact with files and directories. This hands-on approach can be invaluable for resolving complex issues that require a closer look at the compute environment.

The SSH protocol is used to securely connect to remote servers and devices, providing a safe channel for communication over potentially insecure networks. SSH relies on public-key cryptography for authentication, ensuring that data transmitted between the client and server is encrypted and secure. This makes SSH an invaluable tool for tasks such as managing servers, transferring files, and debugging remote compute instances, especially in environments like Azure Machine Learning.

Use the following command to SSH into your compute:

```
ssh azureuser@<public-ip> -p <port-number>
```

In this command, `azureuser` is the username configured for your compute instance, `<public-ip>` is the IP address of your compute target, and `<port-number>` is the port on which the SSH service is listening. By default, SSH uses port 22, but custom configurations might use a different port for enhanced security through obscurity.

For even more secure access, setting up an SSH public-private key pair is highly recommended. This involves generating a key pair on your local machine and then placing the public key on the compute instance. This setup ensures that only someone with the corresponding private key can authenticate and access the instance. Here's a basic outline of the steps to set up an SSH key pair:

1. Generate an SSH key pair on your local machine:

   ```
   ssh-keygen -t rsa -b 4096 -C your_email@example.com
   ```

   This command creates a new RSA key pair with a 4096-bit encryption, and you can follow the prompts to save the key to a secure location and optionally add a passphrase for additional security.

2. Copy the public key to your Azure ML compute instance:

   ```
   ssh-copy-id azureuser@<public-ip> -p <port-number>
   ```

3. Alternatively, you can manually add the public key to the ~/.ssh/authorized_keys file on the remote instance.

When working in more complex network environments, such as those with multiple layers of security, jump servers (or bastion hosts) are often used. A jump server acts as an intermediary between your local machine and the target compute instance. This means you first SSH into the jump server and then from the jump server to the target instance. For example:

```
ssh -J jumpuser@<jump-server-ip> azureuser@<compute-public-ip> -p <port-number>
```

Here, `-J` specifies the jump server, `jumpuser@<jump-server-ip>` is the login for the jump server, and `azureuser@<compute-public-ip>` with `-p <port-number>` specifies the target compute instance.

Using SSH in this manner ensures that your connection is secure, providing robust protection against potential security threats. The SSH protocol itself is designed to provide confidentiality and integrity of data over an unsecured network, utilizing strong encryption algorithms to safeguard the transmitted data. Additionally, features like port forwarding allow you to securely tunnel network services, which can be particularly useful when working with firewalled or restricted environments.

Configure an environment for a job run

In Azure Machine Learning, configuring and submitting training jobs involves setting up the environment and parameters to ensure that your machine learning models are trained efficiently and effectively. This process is essential for executing training jobs, which are tasks that train machine learning models using specified datasets and algorithms. Here's a summary of how to configure the environment and parameters for a training job in Azure Machine Learning:

1. **Create an Experiment**   An experiment in Azure Machine Learning is a logical container for organizing your training runs. It helps in tracking the versioning of models and code.

2. **Select a Compute Target**   The compute target specifies where the training job will be executed. It can be your local machine or a cloud-based compute resource like an Azure ML Compute Cluster.

3. **Create an Environment**   The environment defines the software settings, Python packages, and other dependencies required for your training script. Azure ML allows you to use prebuilt environments or create custom ones.

Define the environment where your machine learning training happens. You can use a predefined Azure Machine Learning environment or create your own. The environment specifies the Python packages, Docker image, environment variables, and software settings for your training and scoring scripts. A full list of environments can be found at https://ml.azure.com/ registries/azureml/environment.

```
from azureml.core import Environment
myenv = Environment.get(workspace=ws, name="AzureML-Minimal")
```

When you create a `ScriptRunConfig`, this configuration specifies the compute target, environment, source directory, and script to run. You can also pass additional arguments to your training script using the arguments parameter.

```
from azureml.core import ScriptRunConfig
src = ScriptRunConfig(source_directory=project_folder,
script='train.py',
 compute_target=my_compute_target,
 environment=myenv)
```

4. **Submit the Experiment**   Use the submit method of the experiment object to submit the training job. You can monitor the job's progress and view the output once the job is complete.

```
run = experiment.submit(config=src)
run.wait_for_completion(show_output=True)
```

Remember to ensure that your training script and any necessary packages are available in the environment where the script runs. If running locally, you're responsible for setting up the Python environment with all required dependencies. If using a remote compute target, you can specify the dependencies in the Azure Machine Learning environment configuration.

Define parameters for a job

In Azure Machine Learning, a job is a single execution of a training script or a pipeline, typically associated with training a machine learning model. Jobs are used to automate and scale machine learning tasks, such as model training, hyperparameter tuning, and model evaluation.

To submit a training job in Azure Machine Learning, you need to set up the environment, specify the parameters, and create a `ScriptRunConfig` object. Imagine you're training a machine learning model to classify images. You have a training script train.py that takes command-line arguments for the learning rate and the number of epochs:

```
from azureml.core import ScriptRunConfig

# Define script parameters
script_params = {
    '--learning-rate': 0.01,
    '--epochs': 10
}

# Create a ScriptRunConfig
src = ScriptRunConfig(source_directory='.',
script='train.py',
 arguments=[f'{k} {v}' for k, v in script_params.items()],
 compute_target=compute_target,
environment=env)

#Submit the experiment:
run = experiment.submit(config=src)
run.wait_for_completion(show_output=True)
```

In this scenario, the training job is configured to run the train.py script with specified learning rate and epochs on the chosen compute target using the defined environment. By submitting this job, Azure Machine Learning will execute the script with the provided parameters, and you can monitor the progress and results of your training run in Azure ML Studio by looking at the job run logs we covered earlier in this chapter.

In the process of developing a machine learning model, one of the first steps is exploring and understanding the data you're working with. Skill 2.1 focuses on the exploration of data using Azure Machine Learning's data assets and data stores. This skill is essential for data scientists and analysts who need to access, wrangle, and prepare data for model training. By mastering these techniques, you'll be able to create a solid foundation for building accurate and efficient machine learning models.

Skill 3.2: Implement training pipelines

Implementing training pipelines in Azure Machine Learning is a critical skill for building robust, scalable, and repeatable machine learning workflows. Pipelines allow you to automate and orchestrate various stages of the machine learning process, from data preparation and training to validation and deployment. By structuring your workflow into discrete, manageable steps, you can enhance collaboration, improve efficiency, and ensure consistency across your projects. This structured approach not only simplifies complex workflows but also makes them easier to debug and maintain.

Configuring job run settings in your scripts is an important process of configuring training pipelines. This involves specifying the compute resources, environment dependencies, and runtime parameters needed for each step of your pipeline. Proper configuration ensures that each component of your pipeline executes correctly and efficiently, leveraging the appropriate resources and settings. Moreover, setting up job run settings effectively can help you manage costs and optimize performance by using the right type of compute target for different tasks.

Creating and managing pipelines in Azure ML also involves several essential tasks. These include creating the pipeline itself, passing data between different steps, and running or scheduling the pipeline to execute at specified times. Additionally, you may need to create custom components to handle unique tasks within your workflow. Using component-based pipelines can further modularize and streamline your process, making it easier to manage and update individual components without disrupting the entire pipeline. By mastering these skills, you can build flexible and powerful machine learning pipelines that support continuous integration and deployment, enhancing the overall productivity and scalability of your machine learning projects.

This skill covers how to:

- Create a pipeline
- Pass data between steps in a pipeline
- Run and schedule a pipeline
- Monitor pipeline runs
- Create custom components
- Use component-based pipelines

Create a pipeline

We've been able to use an abstraction called a job to create runs. A job is used to perform tasks such as integrating MLflow, setting up experiment tracking, and debugging and logging runs. You might be asking why another abstraction, a pipeline, is needed at all. Later in this chapter, the UI will be explored as a way to visually create a pipeline. So what is a pipeline, how is it different from a job, and why are they needed?

Azure Machine Learning pipelines are different from jobs in that pipelines represent an independently executable workflow of a complete machine learning task, whereas jobs are individual tasks within that workflow. In practical machine learning scenarios, solutions are composed of multiple interconnected tasks. For instance, the model training process encompasses a series of tasks such as data ingestion, feature engineering, partitioning data into training and validation sets, and conducting hyperparameter tuning by training multiple models in parallel across a grid of parameters. Additionally, model selection and validation are often performed within a cross-validation loop to ensure robust performance estimation and prevent overfitting. This is why we call this a training pipeline. In fact, each step of the pipeline may have different workloads and thus may require a range of compute resources that appropriately maps to those workloads. Figure 3-4 shows an example of an end-to-end training pipeline for a computer vision task.

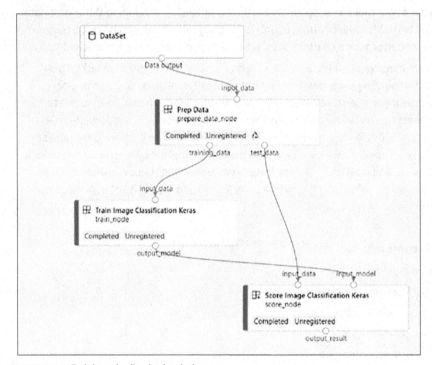

FIGURE 3-4 Training pipeline in the designer

Pipelines are needed to standardize best practices, enable scalable execution, and improve model building efficiency by breaking down the machine learning process into manageable steps, each of which can be developed, optimized, configured, and automated individually. This modular approach facilitates collaboration among different teams, enhances training efficiency, and reduces costs by reusing outputs from previous runs and allocating resources more effectively. With this in mind, how do we work with a pipeline?

Introducing YAML for creating pipelines

YAML (YAML Ain't Markup Language) is a human-readable data serialization format commonly used for configuration files and in applications where data is being stored or transmitted. In the context of Azure Machine Learning, YAML files are used to define the structure of machine learning pipelines and components.

Custom components allow you to extend the functionality of your pipelines by incorporating specialized tasks tailored to your specific requirements. These components can range from bespoke data processing steps to unique model training algorithms. By integrating custom components, you can build more flexible and powerful pipelines that cater to the unique needs of your data science projects. This approach not only improves the adaptability of your workflows but also enables you to leverage advanced techniques and innovations in your machine learning solutions.

When we build a custom component (for example, in a later section you will see how to build a custom pipeline component), your component should have a YAML file defining its metadata, interface, and execution details, and a Python file (or other code files) containing the execution logic—for example, a train.yml file for a training component and a train.py file with the training code.

A pipeline YAML file (pipeline.yml) specifies the workflow of a machine learning task by breaking it down into multiple steps, each represented by a component. The file includes:

- **Type** Specifies that the job is a pipeline.
- **Display Name** A human-readable name for the pipeline.
- **Description** A brief description of the pipeline.
- **Jobs** A dictionary of individual jobs to run as steps within the pipeline. Each job is a reference to a component and includes its inputs and outputs.
- **Settings** Configuration settings for the pipeline, such as the default compute target.

Now that we have defined the YAML format, which is similar to JSON (in fact, it's a superset of JSON) we can look at an example pipeline written in YAML:

```
$schema: https://azuremlschemas.azureedge.net/latest/pipelineJob.schema.json
type: pipeline
display_name: Training Pipeline
description: A pipeline for training a machine learning model.

settings:
  default_compute: azureml:cpu-cluster

jobs:
  data_preprocessing:
    type: command
    component: ./components/data_preprocessing.yml
    inputs:
      raw_data: ./data/raw_data.csv

  model_training:
    type: command
    component: ./components/model_training.yml
    inputs:
      processed_data: ${{parent.jobs.data_preprocessing.outputs.processed_data}}

  model_evaluation:
    type: command
    component: ./components/model_evaluation.yml
    inputs:
      trained_model: ${{parent.jobs.model_training.outputs.trained_model}}
```

Each component referenced in the YAML file (e.g., `./components/model_training.yml`) defines the specific commands and configurations for that job. These component files link to the actual Python scripts that perform the required tasks. Here's how you structure a component YAML file and link it to a Python script.

While YAML is a popular choice for defining pipelines in Azure Machine Learning, there are alternatives:

- **Python SDK** You can use the Azure Machine Learning Python SDK to define and run pipelines programmatically. This approach offers more flexibility and is suitable for complex scenarios.

- **Azure Machine Learning Designer** A drag-and-drop interface for creating pipelines without writing code. It's user-friendly but may not offer the same level of customization as YAML or the Python SDK.

Consider a scenario where you're building a training pipeline for a sales forecasting model. The pipeline includes three main steps: data preprocessing, model training, and model evaluation (see Table 3-4).

TABLE 3-4 Pipeline steps and components

Step	Description
Data Preprocessing	Cleans and transforms raw sales data into a format suitable for training. This step is defined as a separate component in its own YAML file.
Model Training	Trains a regression model using the processed data. This step is defined as a separate component in its own YAML file.
Model Evaluation	Evaluates the performance of the trained model on a validation dataset. This step is defined as a separate component in its own YAML file.
Pipeline YAML File	Orchestrates these components, specifying the order of execution and the flow of data between them.

The YAML pipeline example provided earlier defines a machine learning pipeline with three main steps: data preprocessing, model training, and model evaluation. Let's break down each section of the YAML file to understand its components:

- **$schema** Specifies the schema URL for validation, ensuring that the YAML file adheres to the correct format for an Azure Machine Learning pipeline.

- **$type** Indicates that this YAML file defines a pipeline job. This is important because when you submit your YAML file, Azure Machine Learning recognizes it as defining a pipeline and can build the training pipeline according to your specifications.

- **Jobs** Defines the steps (or jobs) of the pipeline, with each job representing a component of the pipeline. A job can have the following additional options including output names and component files:

  - **Name** The name of the first job, responsible for data preprocessing.

  - **Type** Specifies the type of job, which is a command job in this case.

- **Inputs**   For example, raw_data is an input that points to a raw data file.
- **Outputs**   Specifies the names of the output files or datasets generated by this job. These outputs are crucial for passing data to subsequent pipeline steps and are defined within the sub-component files.
- **Component**   Refers to the specific component file that contains the implementation details for the data preprocessing step. This includes scripts or commands that perform the preprocessing tasks.

Pipelines can get be complicated, but having a standard format like YAML to declaratively build the pipeline allows us to handle training pipelines, inference pipelines, and other parts of the data science solution as configuration that can be source controlled, edited, and ultimately deployed to Azure Machine Learning. In the next section, we will look at how you can run the pipeline in the Azure CLI.

Running the pipeline with Azure CLI

Defining your machine learning pipeline in YAML provides a clear and organized way to outline the various steps and components of your workflow. YAML is highly readable and easy to write, making it an ideal choice for specifying complex configurations. By using YAML to define your pipeline, you can encapsulate all the necessary details, such as data inputs, processing steps, and computational resources, in a single, cohesive document. This approach not only enhances the readability and maintainability of your pipeline but also facilitates collaboration among team members.

Once your pipeline is defined in YAML, you can execute it seamlessly using the Azure command line interface (CLI). The command `az ml job create --file pipeline.yml` submits the pipeline job to your Azure Machine Learning workspace. This command instructs Azure ML to parse the YAML file and initiate the pipeline as defined, leveraging the specified resources and configurations. Running pipelines through the Azure CLI offers flexibility and control, allowing you to manage your machine learning workflows directly from your terminal or integrate them into broader automation scripts and CI/CD pipelines.

After submitting the pipeline job, monitoring its progress is essential to ensure that each step executes as expected. Azure Machine Learning Studio provides a user-friendly interface where you can track the status of your pipeline, view logs, and debug any issues that arise. Additionally, you can use further CLI commands to query the status, retrieve logs, and manage the job remotely. This dual capability of graphical and command-line monitoring ensures that you have comprehensive oversight and control over your pipeline, enabling efficient management and troubleshooting of your machine learning workflows. Once you have defined your pipeline in YAML, you can run it using the Azure CLI:

```
az ml job create --file pipeline.yml
```

This command submits the pipeline job to your Azure Machine Learning workspace. You can monitor the progress of the job in Azure Machine Learning Studio or by using additional CLI commands.

Pass data between steps in a pipeline

Pipelines orchestrate multiple steps, and each of these steps may produce or consume data assets. In our example of a training pipeline, we saw that we could define data assets as inputs and outputs in a job. One common requirement in a production pipeline is passing data between steps. There are many patterns you can use to pass data between steps in a pipeline, but in Azure Machine Learning we follow these steps:

1. Pass the Dataset to Your Script: Decide on the type of dataset to use: `TabularDataset` or `FileDataset`. Use the `as_named_input()` method of the `Dataset` object to pass the dataset's path to your script, creating a `DatasetConsumptionConfig` object. Choose Access Mode (For `FileDataset` Only): Use `as_mount()` if your script accesses a subset of the dataset or if the dataset is too large for your compute resource's disk, as this mode streams the data at runtime. Use `as_download()` if your script processes all the files in your dataset and the disk on your compute resource is large enough, because this mode downloads the dataset to your compute resource, avoiding the overhead of streaming.

2. Pass the Dataset to Your Pipeline Step: Use `TabularDataset.as_named_input()` or `FileDataset.as_named_input()` to create a `DatasetConsumptionConfig` object, and for `FileDataset`, set the access mode using `as_mount()` or `as_download()`. Pass the datasets to your pipeline steps using either the arguments or the inputs argument.

Here is an example using the Python SDK to work with tabu:

```
train_step = PythonScriptStep(
 name="creditcard_defaults",
 script_name="train.py",
 compute_target=cluster,
 inputs=[iris_dataset.as_named_input('iris')]
)
```

You can also use methods such as `random_split()` and `take_sample()` to create multiple inputs or reduce the amount of data passed to your pipeline step. Here's one more example of this technique:

```
seed = 42 # PRNG seed
smaller_dataset = credit_default_dataset.take_sample(0.1, seed=seed) # 10%
train, test = smaller_dataset.random_split(percentage=0.8, seed=seed)

train_step = PythonScriptStep(
 name="train_job",
 script_name="train.py",
 compute_target=cluster,
 inputs=[train.as_named_input('train'), test.as_named_input('test')]
)
```

We can replace the values for all these arguments (e.g., `"train_job"`, `"train.py"`, `cluster`, `iris_dataset`) with your own data. The above snippets just show the form of the call and are not part of a Microsoft sample. We can do the same process in the designer, as shown in Figure 3-5.

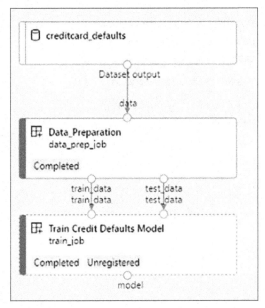

FIGURE 3-5 Passing data between steps

NEED MORE REVIEW? **MOVING DATA IN AND OUT OF PIPELINES**

You can read more about more about moving data in and out of a pipeline here: *https://learn.microsoft.com/en-us/azure/machine-learning/how-to-move-data-in-out-of-pipelines*

We can now build an Azure Machine Learning pipeline and pass data between steps in the pipeline and even use methods to reduce the data that is passed. In the next section, we will look at how we can run and schedule a pipeline.

Run and schedule a pipeline

One crucial aspect of the process of training and deploying machine learning models is the ability to schedule pipeline jobs, which can automate routine tasks such as retraining models and batch predictions. In this guide, we'll explore how to programmatically schedule a pipeline to run on Azure and manage these schedules effectively.

Imagine you're working on a machine learning project that involves predicting customer churn for a subscription-based service. To keep your model up to date with the latest data, you need to retrain it regularly. Instead of manually triggering the retraining process every week, you decide to automate this task by scheduling a pipeline job in Azure Machine Learning.

To schedule a pipeline job, you need to create a schedule that associates a job with a trigger. The trigger can be based on a cron expression or a recurrence pattern. Here's how you can create a time-based schedule with a recurrence pattern using the Azure CLI:

```
$schema: https://azuremlschemas.azureedge.net/latest/schedule.schema.json
name: weekly_retraining_schedule
display_name: Weekly Retraining Schedule
description: Retrain the churn prediction model every week

trigger:
  type: recurrence
  frequency: week
  interval: 1
  schedule:
    days: [sunday]
    hours: [3]
    minutes: [0]
  start_time: "2024-04-07T03:00:00"
  time_zone: "Pacific Standard Time"

create_job: ./retrain_pipeline_job.yml
```

In this example, the pipeline job is scheduled to run every Sunday at 3:00 AM Pacific Standard Time. You might ask what kind of schedules are available and how does it map to your particular use case—for example, if you have decided your training pipeline needs to run on a specific schedule to retrain your model, this is possible using a standard schedule.

Types of schedules

Defining your machine learning pipeline in YAML is just the beginning of creating an efficient and scalable workflow. Once your pipeline is established, the next step is to ensure that it runs consistently and at the appropriate times. Scheduling and running pipelines on a scheduler are crucial in a business context, as they ensure that your machine learning models are trained, validated, and updated regularly, without requiring manual intervention. This automated approach enhances productivity, reduces the risk of errors, and ensures that your models remain accurate and up to date with the latest data.

Azure Machine Learning supports various types of schedules to trigger your pipeline jobs, allowing you to tailor the execution to meet your specific business needs. Recurrence schedules are particularly useful, as they trigger the job based on a specified frequency, such as daily, weekly, or monthly intervals. Additionally, you can define detailed schedules that specify exact hours, minutes, and weekdays for more precise control over when your pipelines run.

On the other hand, a cron uses a cron expression to describe the schedule. For example, "0 3 * * 0" would trigger the job every Sunday at 3:00 AM.

After creating a schedule, you can manage it using the Azure CLI or SDK. Table 3-5 summarizes some of these common tasks with examples.

TABLE 3-5 Commands for managing machine learning schedules

Example Command	Task
`az ml schedule list`	List schedules
`az ml schedule show -n weekly_retraining_schedule`	Check schedule details for `weekly_retraining_schedule`
`az ml schedule update -n weekly_retraining_schedule --set description="Updated description"`	Update the description of `weekly_retraining_schedule`
`az ml schedule disable -n weekly_retraining_schedule`	Disable `weekly_retraining_schedule`
`az ml schedule enable -n weekly_retraining_schedule`	Enable `weekly_retraining_schedule`
`az ml schedule delete -n weekly_retraining_schedule`	Delete `weekly_retraining_schedule`

When your pipeline runs periodically on a schedule, whether it be a cron schedule or a recurrence schedule, you will need some way to monitor the pipeline runs.

Monitor pipeline runs

In this section, we will look at a practical use case for monitoring pipeline runs so you can get an idea of how to design a solution for monitoring in the real world.

Imagine you are developing a sentiment analysis model for social media posts. You already have one or more pipelines to preprocess the data (creating features), train the model from the features, and evaluate the accuracy of the model. To ensure the model's performance and reliability, you need to monitor the pipeline runs that preprocess the data, train the model, and evaluate its accuracy. You decide to use Azure Application Insights to collect and analyze the logs from your Azure Machine Learning pipeline runs.

Setting up logging with Application Insights

Before setting up logging with Application Insights, you should have created an Azure Machine Learning workspace, set up your first pipeline, and installed the Azure Machine Learning SDK per the instructions in Chapter 1. You can use the OpenCensus Azure Monitor Exporter package; Figure 3-6 shows several components of Application Insights and how they interact.

Integrating Azure Machine Learning with Application Insights is essential for building robust data science solutions. Application Insights offers powerful monitoring and diagnostic capabilities that enhance your understanding of how machine learning models and pipelines perform in production. Creating an Application Insights instance and obtaining the connection string allows comprehensive tracking of metrics, logs, and custom events, which are vital for optimizing and maintaining data science workflows.

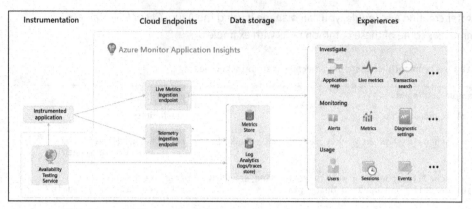

FIGURE 3-6 The logic model diagram for Application Insights components

Begin by navigating to the Azure portal and selecting Create A Resource. Search for Application Insights and follow the prompts to set up a new instance. After the instance is created, obtain the connection string from the Overview or Properties section of the Application Insights resource. This connection string links your Azure Machine Learning workspace with Application Insights, enabling seamless integration and data flow between the two services.

Configuring your Azure Machine Learning experiments to send telemetry data to Application Insights provides valuable information, including real-time performance metrics, error logs, and custom events. For instance, you can track the latency and throughput of model predictions, identify bottlenecks in your pipeline, and monitor resource utilization. These insights allow for proactive management of data science solutions, ensuring efficient and effective operation, which ultimately leads to more reliable and accurate machine learning outcomes.

Configure logging in your pipeline

Logging in a pipeline is a fundamental aspect of managing and debugging machine learning workflows, especially in a cloud environment like Azure Machine Learning. Effective logging provides visibility into the various stages of your pipeline, allowing you to track the progress of your tasks, capture errors, and record key metrics. In the context of data science, this level of detail is invaluable for understanding how your models are performing, identifying issues, and ensuring that your workflows are running smoothly.

Setting up comprehensive logging in your Azure Machine Learning pipeline involves configuring each step to output relevant logs. These logs can capture a wide range of information, from simple print statements to detailed system metrics and error messages. By directing these logs to a centralized location, such as Azure Log Analytics or Application Insights (Azure Log Analytics is used for centralized log management and analysis, while Azure Application Insights focuses on monitoring performance, availability, and usage), you gain a unified view of your pipeline's performance. This centralized logging approach is particularly beneficial in cloud environments, where resources are distributed and tasks are often executed asynchronously.

Logging in a cloud environment is vital for several reasons. First, it enables real-time monitoring and alerting, allowing you to quickly respond to issues as they arise. This capability is essential for maintaining the reliability and performance of your data science solutions. Second, logs provide a historical record of pipeline executions, which can be used for auditing, compliance, and retrospective analysis. This historical data helps in identifying patterns, diagnosing recurring issues, and making informed decisions about optimizations and improvements. In the context of Azure Machine Learning, effective logging practices ensure that your machine learning workflows are transparent, traceable, and resilient, ultimately leading to more robust and trustworthy data science outcomes.

We will need to use a Python script step for logging. You can add the step to your pipeline and configure the connection string as follows:

1. Add a `PythonScriptStep` to your Azure Machine Learning pipeline; we will use it for logging.

2. Configure your `RunConfiguration` with the dependency on `opencensus-ext-azure`.

3. Set the `APPLICATIONINSIGHTS_CONNECTION_STRING` environment variable in your `RunConfiguration`.

Here is an example of Python code for this script step:

```
from azureml.core.runconfig import RunConfiguration
from azureml.pipeline.steps import PythonScriptStep
from azureml.core.conda_dependencies import CondaDependencies
dependencies = CondaDependencies()
dependencies.add_pip_package("opencensus-ext-azure>=1.0.1")

run_config = RunConfiguration(conda_dependencies=dependencies)
run_config.environment.environment_variables = {
  "APPLICATIONINSIGHTS_CONNECTION_STRING": 'InstrumentationKey=your_instrumentation_key'
}

sample_step = PythonScriptStep(
 script_name="sample_step.py",
 compute_target=compute_target,
runconfig=run_config
)
```

Once we have the script step, we need to implement logging in the script step. You can accomplish this by importing the `AzureLogHandler` (which writes the logs) and adding this log handler to the Python logger. The following code block shows how to create a logger object using the logging module and configuring a handler:

```
from opencensus.ext.azure.log_exporter import AzureLogHandler
import logging
logger = logging.getLogger(__name__)
logger.setLevel(logging.DEBUG)
logger.addHandler(logging.StreamHandler())
logger.addHandler(AzureLogHandler())
logger.warning("This log will be sent to Application Insights")
```

Logging with custom dimensions

What about custom dimensions to create structured logging? To provide context to your log messages, you can add custom dimensions such as `parent_run_id`, `step_id`, `step_name`, `experiment_name`, and `run_url`.

```
from azureml.core import Run
run = Run.get_context(allow_offline=False)
custom_dimensions = {
 "parent_run_id": run.parent.id,
 "step_id": run.id,
 "step_name": run.name,
 "experiment_name": run.experiment.name,
"run_url": run.parent.get_portal_url(),
"run_type": "training"
}
logger.info("Log with Custom Dimensions", extra={"custom_dimensions":
custom_dimensions})
```

Custom dimensions are a powerful feature for creating structured logging in Azure Machine Learning, adding valuable context to your log messages. By incorporating custom dimensions such as `parent_run_id`, `step_id`, `step_name`, `experiment_name`, and `run_url`, you can enrich your logs with detailed metadata that makes them easier to search, filter, and analyze. These custom dimensions help you understand the broader context in which each log entry was generated, providing insights into the specific parts of your pipeline and how they relate to the overall workflow.

For example, including a `parent_run_id` in your logs allows you to trace all activities back to the main pipeline run, offering a complete view of the execution flow. The `step_id` and `step_name` dimensions help pinpoint exactly which step in the pipeline generated the log entry, which is particularly useful for identifying where errors or performance bottlenecks occur. By tagging each log with the `experiment_name`, you can easily group and compare logs from different experiments, facilitating cross-experiment analysis and debugging.

Additionally, the `run_url` dimension provides direct links to Azure Machine Learning Studio, where you can view more detailed information about each run. This integration enhances the efficiency of your debugging process, allowing you to quickly navigate from a log entry to the corresponding run details in the Azure ML interface. By leveraging these custom dimensions, you create a structured logging framework that not only improves the granularity and clarity of your logs but also significantly enhances your ability to manage and optimize your machine learning workflows in a cloud environment.

Structured logging with custom dimensions is particularly important in cloud environments for several reasons. First, it improves the manageability of logs by enabling more sophisticated querying and analysis. When dealing with large volumes of log data, being able to filter logs based on specific dimensions such as `experiment_name` or `step_name` can save considerable time and effort. Second, structured logs facilitate better integration with monitoring and alerting systems. For instance, you can set up alerts based on specific log dimensions to notify you of issues related to particular steps or experiments. This proactive approach to monitoring helps ensure the reliability and performance of your data science solutions.

Incorporating custom dimensions into your logging strategy also supports compliance and auditing requirements. By maintaining detailed and structured logs, you can provide a clear and comprehensive audit trail of your machine learning workflows. This transparency is crucial for regulatory compliance and for building trust with stakeholders who rely on your data science solutions. In the context of Azure Machine Learning, structured logging with custom dimensions not only enhances the technical robustness of your workflows but also contributes to their overall credibility and accountability.

Querying logs in Application Insights

Once your pipeline runs are logged to Application Insights, you gain powerful capabilities for querying and analyzing your logs. Application Insights provides features to access your logs under categories like `'traces'` and `'exceptions'`, allowing you to filter and dissect log data efficiently. This granularity is particularly useful in a data science context, where understanding the intricacies of your machine learning workflows can significantly impact model performance and reliability. By leveraging these features, you can track the behavior of your pipeline runs, pinpoint issues, and gather insights to refine your processes.

Using custom dimensions enhances the value of your log data by enabling more-targeted queries. For example, you can filter logs by `parent_run_id`, `step_id`, or `experiment_name` to isolate logs related to specific runs, steps, or experiments. This focused approach allows you to drill down into particular areas of interest, making it easier to identify and address problems. For instance, if you want to examine logs for a specific `parent_run_id`, you can use a query like `traces | where customDimensions.parent_run_id == 'your_parent_run_id'`. Such queries help you navigate through vast amounts of log data to find relevant information quickly, facilitating more efficient debugging and performance tuning.

Now that we understand how to do custom logging, we can look at adding custom components to our pipeline.

Create custom components

Creating custom components in Azure Machine Learning pipelines allows you to encapsulate and modularize your machine learning tasks, making your workflows more flexible, reusable, and easier to manage. In this section, we'll walk you through the process of creating and using custom components in your Azure Machine Learning pipelines.

Azure Machine Learning pipelines are workflows that stitch together various machine learning tasks, such as data preprocessing, model training, and evaluation, into a cohesive process. Components are the building blocks of these pipelines. They represent individual tasks and can be reused across different pipelines. Azure Machine Learning supports two types of components: classic prebuilt components (v1) and custom components (v2). While classic components are mainly for data processing and traditional machine learning tasks, custom components allow you to wrap your own code and logic into reusable components. Figure 3-7 shows the types of components, including metadata, interface, command, code, and environment.

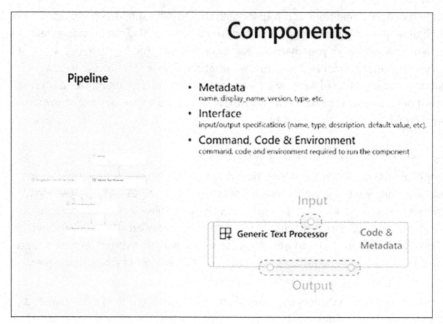

FIGURE 3-7 Diagram of a custom component

EXAM TIP

For new projects, it's recommended to use custom components because they are compatible with Azure ML V2 and will continue to receive updates.

Before you start, make sure you have an Azure subscription and an Azure Machine Learning workspace set up, in addition to the following:

- The Azure CLI extension for Machine Learning installed.

- The examples repository cloned: `git clone https://github.com/Azure/azureml-examples --depth 1`.

To use custom components in your pipelines, you first need to register them in your Azure Machine Learning workspace. This allows you to share and reuse components within the workspace. Registration also supports automatic versioning, ensuring that older pipelines continue to work even when components are updated.

In your Azure Machine Learning workspace, navigate to the Components page and select New Component. Upload the folder containing your component files and select the YAML file to register the component. Repeat this process for any additional components you want to register. Another way is to create custom components in the designer by clicking Components, located under Assets in the studio. Figure 3-8 shows the webpage associated with components.

FIGURE 3-8 Creating custom components in the designer

Use component-based pipelines

Once your components are registered (see Figure 3-9), you can create a pipeline that uses them. You can create a new pipeline. In Azure Machine Learning Studio, create a new pipeline and select the Custom option. Give your pipeline a meaningful name.

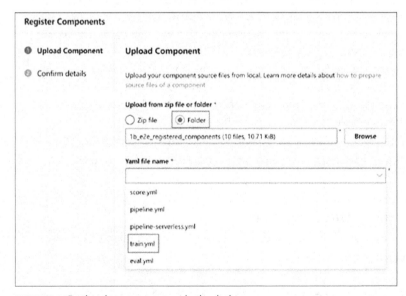

FIGURE 3-9 Registering a component in the designer

Next, you can add components to the pipeline by finding your registered components in the asset library under the Components tab. Drag and drop them onto the pipeline canvas. Connect them appropriately to define the flow of data and execution. Alternatively, you can create a new pipeline with custom components, as in Figure 3-10.

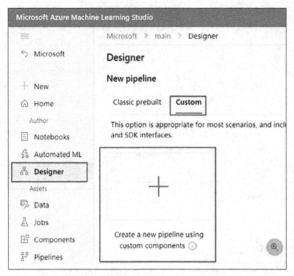

FIGURE 3-10 Creating a pipeline with custom components

Double-click a component to configure its parameters, inputs, and outputs. You can promote important parameters to the pipeline level for easier access when running the pipeline. The concept of promoting parameters to the pipeline level is important because you want to streamline the process of adjusting key variables, making it more efficient to modify and manage them without having to configure each individual component. This practice enhances the flexibility and scalability of your pipeline, allowing for easier experimentation and optimization. It also ensures consistency across different runs, since you can centrally manage and update parameters that affect multiple components within the pipeline.

Once your pipeline is configured, click Configure & Submit to submit it for execution. Follow the prompts to configure the experiment, job display name, inputs/outputs, and runtime settings.

> **NEED MORE REVIEW?** **CUSTOM PIPELINE COMPONENTS**
>
> Custom pipeline components are detailed here: *https://learn.microsoft.com/en-us/azure/ machine-learning/concept-component*.

Skill 3.3: Manage models in Azure Machine Learning

Mastering the implementation of training pipelines is a critical aspect of effective machine learning operations. This section delves into several key skills necessary for optimizing your pipelines in Azure Machine Learning. These skills include configuring job run settings for scripts, describing MLflow model output, identifying the appropriate framework to package a model, and assessing a model using responsible AI guidelines. Each of these components plays a vital role in ensuring that your machine learning models are not only accurate and efficient but also ethical and sustainable.

The first skill we will explore is configuring job run settings for a script. Properly setting up job run parameters is fundamental to ensuring that your machine learning tasks execute smoothly and efficiently. This includes defining the compute resources, environment dependencies, and runtime configurations that your script requires. By carefully configuring these settings, you can optimize the performance of your pipeline, manage costs, and ensure that each step in your workflow runs under the best possible conditions. Understanding how to tailor these settings to your specific needs is essential for maximizing the effectiveness of your machine learning projects.

Next, we will discuss how to describe MLflow model output. MLflow is a powerful tool for managing the lifecycle of machine learning models, from experimentation to deployment. Being able to accurately describe and interpret MLflow model outputs is crucial for tracking the performance and evolution of your models. This involves understanding the various metrics and artifacts that MLflow generates, as well as how to use these outputs to inform decisions about model tuning and improvement. Additionally, we will cover the importance of choosing the right framework to package your model. The choice of framework can significantly impact the ease of deployment, scalability, and maintainability of your model. We will guide you through the considerations for selecting a packaging framework that aligns with your project requirements and deployment environment.

Finally, we will delve into the principles of assessing a model using responsible AI guidelines. As machine learning becomes increasingly integral to business operations and decision-making, it is crucial to ensure that models are developed and deployed responsibly. Responsible AI encompasses a range of practices designed to mitigate biases, ensure transparency, and uphold ethical standards in AI development. We will examine how to assess your models against these guidelines, ensuring that they not only perform well but also align with broader societal and ethical considerations. This holistic approach to model assessment is vital for building trust and accountability in AI systems.

By mastering these skills, you will be well-equipped to create and manage robust, efficient, and ethical machine learning pipelines in Azure Machine Learning. Each topic we cover will provide you with practical insights and techniques to enhance the quality and integrity of your data science projects, ensuring that they deliver valuable and responsible outcomes.

This skill covers how to:

- Describe MLflow model output
- Identify an appropriate framework to package a model
- Assess a model by using responsible AI guidelines

Describe MLflow model output

MLflow is a versatile open-source platform that streamlines the entire machine learning lifecycle, including experimentation, reproducibility, and deployment. When combined with Azure Machine Learning, MLflow offers an enhanced experience for managing and tracking your machine learning projects.

MLflow's integration with Azure Machine Learning allows you to utilize MLflow's tracking, model management, and deployment features within the Azure ecosystem. This integration enables you to:

- Use Azure Machine Learning workspaces as your MLflow tracking server, centralizing the logging of metrics, parameters, and artifacts.

- Manage the lifecycle of your MLflow models within Azure Machine Learning, including registration, versioning, and deployment.

Tracking with MLflow

In Azure Machine Learning, MLflow is primarily used for tracking experiments but is also used for storing models, scripts and other artifacts, model versioning, and ensuring that experiments are reproducible. This involves logging various aspects of your machine learning runs, such as metrics, parameters, and artifacts (e.g., models and plots). When you run experiments using MLflow in Azure Machine Learning, all the tracked information is stored in your workspace, making it accessible for analysis and comparison.

MLflow output in Azure Machine Learning

The output from MLflow tracking in Azure Machine Learning includes:

- **Metrics**   Quantitative measures of your model's performance, such as accuracy, precision, recall, or custom metrics defined in your experiments.

- **Parameters**   Configurations and hyperparameters used in your experiments, allowing you to understand how different settings impact model performance.

- **Artifacts**   Files produced during your experiments, including serialized models, plots, and other relevant data. These artifacts are stored in the Azure Machine Learning workspace and can be accessed for further analysis or deployment.

- **Model Registry**   MLflow's open-source tool for experiment tracking and model registration.

Azure Machine Learning supports MLflow for model management, enabling you to register and version your MLflow models within the Azure ecosystem. This allows for streamlined model lifecycle management, from experimentation to deployment.

Model deployment with MLflow

MLflow models can be deployed directly to Azure Machine Learning endpoints, both for real-time and batch inference. The deployment process is simplified, since you don't need to specify an environment or a scoring script. (A scoring script is a file that Azure Machine Learning uses to define the logic and code needed to make a prediction using a trained model.) Azure Machine Learning handles the deployment, making your MLflow models readily available for serving predictions.

Key features of deploying MLflow models in Azure Machine Learning

There are a few key features of deploying MLflow models in Azure Machine Learning. One option is no-code deployment, which allows you to automate the generation of scoring scripts and environments without having to explicitly create the scoring scripts. However, there are many deployment tools available, and knowledge of concepts like package dependencies and model signatures is essential to working with MLflow. Some of these options are described below:

- **No-Code Deployment** Automates the generation of scoring scripts and environments, streamlining the deployment process.
- **Package Dependencies** Ensures that all dependencies specified in the MLflow model are met, adding any required packages for the inferencing server.
- **Model Signatures** Enforces compatibility between the expected inputs (as defined in the model's signature) and the actual data inputs during inference.
- **Deployment Tools** Offers a variety of tools to deploy MLflow models, each with different capabilities and deployment options.

Table 3-6 provides a comparison of the deployment tools available in Azure Machine Learning for deploying MLflow models. Producing an MLflow model and deploying it are two different processes. There is a simple (and no-code) way to deploy models within the MLflow SDK.

TABLE 3-6 Summary of deployment tools

Deployment Tool	Managed Online Endpoints	Batch Endpoints	Web Services (ACI/AKS)	Customization with Scoring Script
MLflow SDK	Yes (Preview)	Not Supported	Legacy Support	Not Supported
Azure Machine Learning CLI/SDK	Yes	Yes	Not Supported	Yes
Azure Machine Learning Studio	Yes	Yes	Not Supported	Yes

Identify an appropriate framework to package a model

Deploying MLflow models to Azure Machine Learning involves several key considerations, especially when working with different machine learning frameworks. Each framework has its own requirements and best practices for logging and deployment.

Imagine you are a data scientist working on a machine learning project that involves multiple models built with different frameworks, including Scikit-learn, TensorFlow, PyTorch,

XGBoost, and a custom framework. You need to deploy these models to Azure Machine Learning for serving predictions in a production environment.

When you log a model, MLflow automatically identifies and fixes the versions of packages in the model's Conda dependencies. However, this automatic detection of packages may not always align with your specific needs or intentions. Therefore, it's advisable to log models with a tailored Conda dependencies definition if the automatic package detection does not meet your requirements. Table 3-7 summarizes some of the logging functions and frameworks.

TABLE 3-7 Logging functions and frameworks

Framework	Logging Function	Deployment Considerations
Scikit-learn	`mlflow.sklearn.log_model`	Ensure all dependencies are correctly specified in the Conda environment for smooth deployment.
TensorFlow	`mlflow.tensorflow.log_model`	Specify the correct version of TensorFlow in the Conda environment to avoid issues during deployment.
PyTorch	`mlflow.pytorch.log_model`	Accurately specify all necessary dependencies and library versions in the Conda environment.
XGBoost	`mlflow.xgboost.log_model`	Ensure the correct version of XGBoost is specified in the Conda environment for successful deployment.
Custom	`mlflow.log_model`	Provide a detailed Conda environment and possibly a custom scoring script to handle the inference process correctly.

In this scenario, you would log each model using the appropriate MLflow logging function for the framework used. Then, you would carefully prepare the Conda environment for each model, ensuring that all necessary dependencies and versions are specified. For custom frameworks, you might need to provide additional configuration or a custom scoring script to ensure correct inference behavior.

Assess a model by using responsible AI guidelines

Assessing a model based on responsible AI guidelines in MLflow involves ensuring that the model adheres to principles such as fairness, reliability, transparency, and privacy. These guidelines are crucial for developing, assessing, and deploying AI systems in a safe, trustworthy, and ethical manner.

Imagine you are a data scientist who has developed a machine learning model using MLflow. You want to deploy this model in Azure Machine Learning but need to ensure that it aligns with responsible AI principles. You will assess the model based on fairness, reliability, transparency, and other guidelines. Table 3-8 summarizes the key considerations for assessing MLflow models based on responsible AI guidelines:

TABLE 3-8 Key considerations for MLflow models

Principle	Description	Tools & Techniques
Fairness and Inclusiveness	Ensure that the model treats all groups fairly and does not discriminate.	Fairness assessment component in Azure Machine Learning's Responsible AI dashboard.
Reliability and Safety	Verify that the model operates reliably and safely under various conditions.	Error analysis component in Azure Machine Learning's Responsible AI dashboard.
Transparency	Ensure that the model's decision-making process is transparent and interpretable.	Model interpretability and counterfactual what-if analysis in Azure Machine Learning's Responsible AI dashboard.
Privacy and Security	Confirm the model complies with privacy laws and safeguards sensitive information.	Differential privacy tools like SmartNoise; encryption and access control in Azure Machine Learning.
Accountability	Maintain accountability for the model's behavior and outcomes.	MLOps capabilities in Azure Machine Learning for tracking the model's lifecycle.

Chapter summary

- You can configure compute resources and job settings in Azure Machine Learning to optimize model training scripts and performance.
- You can now integrate and consume data seamlessly from various assets, enhancing data accessibility and utility during job runs.
- You can utilize MLflow for detailed metrics logging and use logs for effective troubleshooting of job run issues.
- You can now automate and manage complex workflows by creating and scheduling training pipelines, improving efficiency and consistency.
- You can design custom components and utilize component-based pipelines to increase modularity and reusability in model training.
- You can streamline model training and management by identifying suitable frameworks for packaging and deploying models.
- You can now effectively manage models in Azure, using MLflow to track outputs and applying responsible AI guidelines to ensure ethical model deployment.

Thought experiment

In this thought experiment, demonstrate your skills and knowledge of the topics covered in this chapter. You can find the answers in the section that follows.

1. Effective Job Configuration in Azure Machine Learning: What is essential for optimizing model training scripts and performance?

   A. Increasing the number of compute instances indiscriminately.

   B. Limiting data access to minimize processing time.

C. Configuring compute resources and job settings appropriately.

D. Avoiding the use of external libraries and tools.

2. Data Integration and Utilization: How can users enhance data accessibility and utility during Azure Machine Learning job runs?

A. By ignoring external data sources and focusing solely on internal datasets.

B. Consuming data only from real-time sources to ensure freshness.

C. Integrating and consuming data seamlessly from various assets.

D. Using manual data entry to avoid integration complexities.

3. Managing and Automating Model Training Workflows: Which approach best describes managing complex workflows in Azure Machine Learning?

A. Scheduling pipelines manually each time a run is needed.

B. Creating and scheduling training pipelines for automated workflow management.

C. Avoiding the use of pipelines to simplify the training process.

D. Using only default components without customization.

4. Which of the following is considered the best practice for ensuring ethical model deployment in Azure Machine Learning according to the Responsible AI Guidelines from Microsoft?

A. Deploying models based on their accuracy and fairness metric.

B. Utilizing MLflow to track outputs while also incorporating a Responsible AI dashboard to conduct fairness assessments, transparency documentation, bias audits, and implementing human-in-the-loop oversight mechanisms.

C. Relying on automated tools and packages to enforce ethical guidelines.

D. Packaging models with any available framework and deploying them universally, assuming they will perform equally well across all environments and use cases without specific suitability assessments.

Thought experiment answers

This section contains the solutions to the thought experiment. Each answer explains why the answer choice is correct.

1. The answer is **C.** Configuring compute resources and job settings appropriately is essential for optimizing model training scripts and performance in Azure Machine Learning. Option A involves indiscriminate use of resources, which is not efficient. Option B limits data access, which could hinder performance rather than enhance it. Option D suggests avoiding external tools, which could reduce the effectiveness and flexibility of the training process.

2. The answer is **C.** Integrating and consuming data seamlessly from various assets enhances data accessibility and utility during job runs, aligning with best practices in

Azure Machine Learning. Option A ignores the benefits of external data sources, reducing the potential for comprehensive data analysis. Option B limits the data to real-time sources only, which is not always necessary or beneficial. Option D, manual data entry, introduces inefficiencies and potential errors.

3. The answer is **B.** Creating and scheduling training pipelines for automated workflow management effectively manages complex workflows in Azure Machine Learning. Option A involves manual scheduling, which is less efficient than automated processes. Option C, avoiding the use of pipelines, would lead to less structured and potentially more error-prone training processes. Option D does not leverage the benefits of customization, which can improve efficiency and performance.

4. The answer is **B**. Utilizing MLflow to track outputs while also incorporating a Responsible AI dashboard to perform fairness assessments, document transparency, conduct bias audits, and implement human-in-the-loop oversight mechanisms This approach ensures ethical model deployment in Azure Machine Learning by comprehensively applying responsible AI guidelines. Option A ignores the review of models' decision-making processes, which is essential for ethical AI. Option C focuses solely on accuracy, overlooking other significant ethical considerations. Option D implies indiscriminate use of frameworks, which may not be suitable for all contexts and could result in deployment compatibility and ethical issues.

## CHAPTER 4

Deploy and retrain a model

Deploying and operating machine learning models within a production environment present unique challenges and require a strategic approach. Unlike traditional software applications, machine learning models necessitate continuous monitoring, frequent updates, and dynamic scaling to handle fluctuating data loads and evolving data patterns. Professionals skilled in machine learning operations (MLOps) take on the critical role of bridging the gap between experimental data science and robust, scalable production systems.

This process requires a meticulous balance between operational demands and the predictive performance of models. It involves translating complex model requirements into a deployable solution that efficiently utilizes compute resources, manages data flow, and adheres to compliance and security standards. Handling machine learning deployments also involves specific practices distinct from conventional software deployment, such as managing data drift, model versioning, and automated retraining cycles. These practices ensure that models remain accurate and relevant as the underlying data changes over time.

With the increasing complexity of models, especially with the proliferation of deep learning and large language models, the operational aspect of machine learning has become more critical. This includes adhering to stricter regulatory requirements and managing the considerable computational resources these models require. Azure Machine Learning provides a robust environment for addressing these challenges through its comprehensive suite of tools and services.

In this chapter, we will explore the crucial stages of deploying and managing machine learning models in Azure. We begin with an overview of how to configure settings for both online and batch deployments, ensuring that models are responsive and scalable. We'll discuss how to deploy models to different endpoints, such as online for real-time predictions and batch for processing large volumes of data (see Figure 4-1).

We'll also cover operational strategies to enhance model performance and reliability. This includes setting up monitoring systems to track model behavior in production, using Azure's capabilities to trigger retraining processes, and applying MLOps practices to automate and streamline model lifecycle management. The integration of Azure DevOps and GitHub for continuous integration and delivery plays a pivotal role in maintaining the agility of machine learning operations.

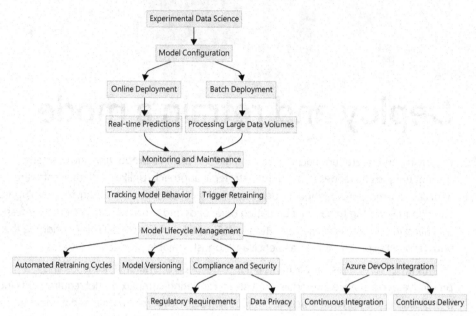

FIGURE 4-1 Deploying and managing machine learning models starting from experimental data science to model configuration and online or batch deployment

By the end of this chapter, you will gain comprehensive insights into deploying and managing machine learning models using Azure Machine Learning, preparing you for the practical challenges of operating these models in real-world scenarios.

EXAM TIP

When preparing for exam questions related to deploying and managing machine learning models, focus on understanding Azure's specific features and recommended practices for MLOps. Questions often probe your ability to choose solutions that not only resolve immediate operational issues but also optimize long-term manageability and cost-efficiency. If choices seem similar, lean toward options that offer better scalability, easier maintenance, and stronger alignment with Azure MLOps frameworks.

Skills covered in this chapter:

- Skill 4.1: Deploy a model
- Skill 4.2: Apply machine learning operations (MLOps) practices

Skill 4.1: Deploy a model

Deploying a model in Azure Machine Learning enables applications to leverage trained models through various endpoints. This deployment is achieved by transitioning a model from a development stage to a production environment where it becomes accessible for real-world applications. Azure Machine Learning supports the creation of both online and batch endpoints, catering to different application needs. Online endpoints are suitable for real-time predictions where low latency responses are essential, while batch endpoints are designed for processing large volumes of data where immediate responses are not necessary.

The process starts with model registration, where the trained model is stored in Azure's version-controlled repository. This step is followed by setting up the environment, which involves specifying all the necessary runtime settings to ensure that the model's behavior remains consistent across different deployment conditions. After the model and its environment are configured, the next step is to select an appropriate deployment target. For instance, Azure Kubernetes Service (AKS) can be utilized for high-scale, high-availability scenarios, whereas Azure Container Instances (ACI) are ideal for lower-scale situations such as development and testing.

Depending on the operational requirements, you may choose between setting up an online or batch endpoint. Online endpoints facilitate immediate responses to API requests, making them ideal for interactive applications. In contrast, batch endpoints handle requests in bulk, processing data as a single batch, which is more efficient for scenarios where the application can tolerate some delay in receiving outputs. Both types of endpoints can be scaled and monitored to ensure optimal performance and reliability. Azure Machine Learning also provides tools for monitoring these endpoints, collecting data on usage, response times, and prediction accuracy to help diagnose issues and assess the model's performance in production. To illustrate the deployment process, consider Table 4-1.

TABLE 4-1 Steps in deploying a model in Azure Machine Learning

Step	Description
Model Registration	Store and manage the model in Azure's version-controlled repository.
Environment Setup	Specify the runtime environment to ensure consistency across deployments.
Deployment Target Selection	Choose between AKS, ACI, or edge devices based on scale, cost, and performance needs.
Endpoint Configuration	Decide between online and batch endpoints depending on the application's latency and volume requirements.
API Creation	Package the model as a web service accessible via an API for making predictions.
Monitoring Setup	Utilize Azure's tools to track performance and health of the deployed model.

EXAM TIP

Understanding the differences between online and batch endpoints, along with their appropriate use cases, is essential for effectively deploying machine learning models in Azure. Familiarity with the setup and management of these endpoints ensures that deployed models meet the specific needs of different applications, maintaining performance and accuracy over time.

Before you start, make sure you have an Azure subscription and an Azure Machine Learning workspace set up.

> **This skill covers how to:**
> - Configure settings for online deployment
> - Configure the compute for a batch deployment
> - Deploy a model to an online endpoint
> - Deploy a model to a batch endpoint
> - Test an online deployed service
> - Invoke the batch endpoint to start a batch scoring job

Configure settings for online deployment

In Azure Machine Learning, deploying machine learning models for inferencing can be done using two main methods: online deployment and batch deployment. These deployment options are tailored to suit specific application needs and performance requirements, making it crucial to understand the distinctions and capabilities of each.

Online deployment is ideal for scenarios where instant predictions are necessary and where low latency is a requirement. This method involves setting up a predictive service that responds in real-time to API requests. Following is a list some of the key configuration options for online deployment:

> *IMPORTANT* **BASH ON WINDOWS SUBSYSTEM FOR LINUX (WSL)**
>
> The CLI examples in this section assume you are using the Bash (or compatible) shell—for example, from a Linux system or Windows Subsystem for Linux.

- **Instance Type** Choose between CPU or GPU-based virtual machines.
  Influences the performance and cost of the deployment.
- **Instance Count** Determines the number of instances available to handle incoming requests.
  Impacts scalability and fault tolerance.
- **Autoscaling** Automatically adjusts the number of instances based on traffic patterns.
  Optimizes resource utilization and cost.
- **Authentication Mode** Supports key-based or token-based authentication.
  Ensures secure access to the deployment endpoint.
- **Traffic Rules** Manages how traffic is distributed across multiple deployments.
  Useful for A/B testing or implementing blue-green deployment strategies.

- **Environment**   Specifies the Docker image and Conda environment.

Guarantees that the deployment has the correct runtime dependencies.

It is important to note that while choosing an online deployment is ideal in situations where low latency is required, you should assess whether it is really required since choosing this option is not without trade-offs. One trade-off is that features must be available at the time of prediction. The model you build—regardless of whether it is a classification, regression, or some other problem type—was trained on some features that are required to make an inference.

Another important consideration for these deployment options involves scalability. Here, an online endpoint with autoscaling capabilities is important for handling real-time product recommendations and other types of online deployments for which a customer expects low latency from your system. This setup ensures that the system maintains low latency, even during peak traffic periods, such as holiday sales or special promotions.

Consider an e-commerce website that experiences variable daily traffic patterns with significant spikes on weekends and holidays. In order to manage this, the platform utilizes autoscaling.

What is autoscaling? Autoscaling automatically scales the number of virtual machines during traffic spikes to maintain performance without incurring unnecessary costs during off-peak times.

Instance types available

GPU and CPU-based instance types offer different options depending on the traffic types and spikes in traffic. There are also several instance types available. GPU-based instances are used during peak times for faster processing of complex recommendation algorithms. Alternatively, CPU-based instance types can be used during normal traffic periods to reduce costs.

In a real-world data science solution, we might also decide to employ token-based authentication to secure the API endpoints against unauthorized access, ensuring that only legitimate website and app services can request predictions. Table 4-2 summarizes some of the configuration options.

TABLE 4-2   Configuration options for real-time recommendations

Configuration Option	Description	Use Case Impact
Instance Type	Choice of CPU or GPU virtual machines	Affects cost and performance
Instance Count	Number of active instances	Influences scalability and redundancy
Autoscaling	Dynamic adjustment of instance counts	Optimizes costs and resource usage
Authentication Mode	Key-based or token-based security (a key difference being a key doesn't expire but a token does expire)	Secures access to predictive services

Configuration Option	Description	Use Case Impact
Traffic Rules	Distribution management across deployments	Facilitates A/B testing and updates
Environment	Specifies runtime dependencies (Docker, Conda)	Ensures compatibility and performance

Azure Machine Learning's deployment options provide the flexibility and scalability needed to implement robust, real-time predictive services. You should try to understand and properly configure these options since businesses can significantly enhance their operational efficiency and customer engagement by implementing these options as part of your data science solution in Azure.

Introduction to safely rolling out machine learning models in Azure

When deploying machine learning models in production, ensuring a smooth transition without disrupting service is crucial. Azure Machine Learning offers a safe rollout strategy, allowing you to introduce new model versions gradually. Following are the key concepts for understanding and implementing this approach:

- Deploying machine learning models to production in Azure requires careful planning to avoid disruptions.

- A safe rollout strategy, like the blue-green deployment method, allows you to introduce new model versions gradually.

- This approach helps you validate the new model's performance by initially directing a small percentage of traffic to it.

- By carefully monitoring the deployment, you can ensure the new model works as expected before fully transitioning all traffic to it.

- This strategy reduces the risk of errors or downtime when deploying updates to machine learning models in production environments.

In the next section, we will expand on these kinds of strategies to look at production deployment strategies in general and what happens when we deploy updates or changes in a managed online endpoint environment.

Production deployment strategies

When deploying updates or changes in a managed online endpoint environment, a phased approach is commonly used to minimize disruption and risk. For example, updates can be applied to a fraction of the nodes at a time—commonly referred to as *rolling updates*. In such scenarios, if the deployment comprises 10 nodes, the update process would handle 2 nodes at a time, representing 20% of the total deployment. This method allows the service to continue operating with the majority of its capacity while the update is being implemented, thereby reducing downtime and providing a buffer to monitor for any issues that arise with the new configuration before it is fully deployed across all nodes.

In contrast, deployment strategies in a Kubernetes environment typically involve a different approach known as *immutable deployments*. Here, rather than updating existing nodes, the system spins up a new set of nodes (or pods) based on the new configuration and gradually replaces the old nodes. This strategy is often executed using a rolling update mechanism provided by Kubernetes, where new deployment instances are created, and the old ones are systematically phased out. This method ensures that there is always a functioning instance running, thereby minimizing the potential for service interruptions as the deployment transitions from the old configuration to the new one.

For production environments where reliability and seamless transition are critical, the blue-green deployment strategy is highly recommended. In *blue-green deployments*, two identical environments are maintained: one hosting the current live production version (blue) and the other hosting the new version (green). Traffic is initially directed entirely to the blue environment. Once the new version in the green environment is fully tested and ready to go live, the traffic is switched over. This switch can be made almost instantaneously, reducing downtime to nearly zero. Furthermore, if any issues are detected after switching to the green environment, traffic can be quickly reverted back to the blue environment, thus significantly mitigating risks associated with the deployment.

Adopting such advanced deployment strategies ensures that updates and changes can be made to production systems with minimal impact on the end users. Each approach, whether rolling updates in managed endpoints, immutable deployments in Kubernetes, or blue-green deployments for critical production environments, offers specific advantages that can be leveraged depending on the operational requirements and risk tolerance of the business. These methods not only enhance the robustness of deployment processes but also provide safeguards to maintain service continuity and reliability, which are paramount in production settings.

Deploying machine learning models at scale requires a robust and flexible infrastructure that can handle the complexities of real-world applications. Azure Kubernetes Service (AKS) provides a powerful platform for deploying, managing, and scaling machine learning models in production. Leveraging AKS for model deployment offers numerous advantages, including automatic scaling, rolling updates, and seamless integration with other Azure services. This section will explore the key aspects of using AKS to deploy machine learning models, highlighting best practices and practical tips for optimizing your deployment workflow.

Setting up AKS for model deployment with Azure Machine Learning

The first step in deploying machine learning models with AKS is to set up an AKS cluster. This involves creating a Kubernetes cluster in Azure, which will serve as the foundation for your deployment. You can create an AKS cluster through the Azure portal, Azure CLI, or by using infrastructure-as-code tools such as Terraform. When setting up your cluster, consider the following:

- **Cluster Configuration** Define the size and configuration of your cluster based on the expected load and performance requirements. This includes selecting the appropriate node size, number of nodes, and configuring node pools to optimize resource utilization.

- **Networking**   Configure networking settings to ensure secure and efficient communication between your AKS cluster and other Azure services. This includes setting up virtual networks, subnet configurations, and network security groups.
- **Security**   Implement security best practices by enabling role-based access control (RBAC), setting up network policies, and using Azure Active Directory for authentication.

Deploying models as Kubernetes pods

Once your AKS cluster is set up, the next step is to containerize your machine learning model and deploy it as a Kubernetes pod. Containerization involves packaging your model along with its dependencies into a Docker container, ensuring that it can run consistently across different environments. The process typically involves:

- **Creating a Docker Image**   Write a Dockerfile that specifies the base image, dependencies, and the command to run your model. Build the Docker image and push it to a container registry, such as Azure Container Registry (ACR).
- **Defining Kubernetes Resources**   Create Kubernetes resource files (YAML) to define the deployment and service specifications. These files include details about the container image, resource limits, environment variables, and how the service should be exposed (e.g., via a `LoadBalancer` or `Ingress`).
- **Deploying to AKS**   Use `kubectl` commands or CI/CD pipelines to apply the Kubernetes resource files and deploy your model to the AKS cluster. Monitor the deployment process to ensure that the pods are running successfully and the service is accessible.

Managing and scaling model deployments

One of the key benefits of using AKS is its ability to manage and scale model deployments automatically. AKS provides built-in features to handle scaling, updates, and monitoring, ensuring that your models can meet the demands of production workloads. Key considerations include:

- **Auto-scaling**   Configure horizontal pod autoscaling (HPA) to automatically adjust the number of pods based on CPU or memory utilization. This ensures that your deployment can handle varying loads without manual intervention.
- **Rolling Updates**   Use Kubernetes rolling updates to deploy new versions of your model with minimal downtime. This allows you to update your model while maintaining service availability, gradually shifting traffic to the new version.
- **Monitoring and Logging**   Integrate monitoring and logging solutions such as Azure Monitor, Prometheus, and Grafana to track the performance and health of your model deployments. Set up alerts to notify you of any issues, such as high latency or resource exhaustion.

Integrating with Azure ML and DevOps

For a seamless workflow, integrate AKS deployments with Azure Machine Learning and Azure DevOps. Azure Machine Learning provides tools to automate the deployment process, track model versions, and monitor model performance. Azure DevOps can be used to create CI/CD pipelines that automate the building, testing, and deployment of your models to AKS. This integration ensures a streamlined and efficient deployment pipeline, from model development to production.

In conclusion, deploying machine learning models with Azure Kubernetes Service offers a scalable, reliable, and flexible solution for production workloads. By following best practices for setting up AKS, containerizing models, and managing deployments, you can ensure that your machine learning solutions are robust, maintainable, and capable of meeting the demands of real-world applications.

Configure the compute for a batch deployment

In Azure Machine Learning, batch deployment is another critical method for deploying machine learning models and is particularly useful for scenarios where large volumes of data need to be processed without the need for real-time inferencing. Batch deployments are designed to handle asynchronous processing tasks, allowing for efficient management of computational resources and scheduling flexibility.

Introducing batch deployments

Batch deployment in Azure Machine Learning is optimized for processing jobs where immediate responses are not required. This deployment type is typically used for end-of-day data processing, complex simulations, or scenarios requiring extensive computational resources that can be scheduled during off-peak hours. Like the online deployment scenario, there are several key configuration options for batch deployment in Azure Machine Learning:

- **Compute Target**   Select between Azure Machine Learning compute clusters or attached compute resources.
- **Node Count**   Specifies the number of nodes in the compute cluster and allows parallel processing across multiple instances, enhancing throughput.
- **Max Concurrent Runs**   Limits the number of batch jobs that can run simultaneously (additionally, this option helps manage resource contention and ensures stable performance.)
- **Retention Time**   Sets how long the outputs of batch jobs are retained before they are automatically deleted.
- **Input Data**   Configuration of input datasets or file paths required for batch processing.
- **Output Data**   Specifies the location and format for storing the results of batch jobs.

A practical application of batch deployment can be seen in a healthcare organization that processes a large dataset of patient records overnight. By using a batch endpoint, the organization can efficiently handle extensive data volumes without impacting its day-to-day operations. The results are then stored in Azure Blob Storage for further analysis, such as identifying trends or improving patient care strategies.

In this healthcare example, the organization schedules the batch processing to occur during off-peak hours to optimize resource use and reduce costs. The configuration might include:

- **Compute Target** Utilizes Azure Machine Learning compute clusters specifically upgraded for high-performance tasks.
- **Node Count** Employs multiple nodes to parallelize the processing of patient records, speeding up the task.
- **Retention Time** Sets a retention policy to keep the processed data for a month to comply with healthcare regulations. Table 4-3 summarizes some of these options with a side-by-side comparison of the two deployment models.

TABLE 4-3 Key configuration options and features for deployment types

Feature	Online Deployment	Batch Deployment
Inferencing Type	Real-time	Asynchronous
Instance Type	CPU/GPU options	Compute target selection
Scaling	Autoscaling based on traffic	Node count for parallel processing
Authentication	Key-based or token-based	N/A (usually managed at the compute level)
Traffic Management	Traffic rules for A/B testing	N/A
Environment	Docker image and Conda environment	Conda environment for the compute target
Data Handling	Real-time request processing	Batch input and output data configuration

Deploy a model to an online endpoint

Deploying a model to an online endpoint enables real-time inferencing in Azure Machine Learning. This process involves preparing your system, defining the endpoint and deployment, and deploying the model locally for testing before deploying it to Azure. At this point, you should have a workspace, but in case you don't, there are some prerequisites:

- Azure CLI with the ML extension.
- Azure Machine Learning workspace.

Set your Azure subscription, workspace, and resource group as defaults. Clone the Azure ML examples repository and navigate to the CLI directory.

Define the endpoint

When defining the endpoint, we can specify more than just the endpoint name. We should think about adding the authentication mode (key or token-based), and optionally add a description and tags. When setting up a service endpoint, it is important to specify the endpoint name clearly. This name will be used to identify and access the service across your network. Additionally, you must choose the authentication mode; options include key-based or token-based systems, which help secure the endpoint by ensuring that only authorized users can access the services.

Optionally, you can enhance the configuration by adding a description to the endpoint. This description can provide other users or developers with a clear understanding of the endpoint's purpose and its functionality. This information is particularly helpful in larger projects where multiple endpoints can cause confusion.

Furthermore, adding tags to the endpoint is a useful practice. Tags allow for easier management and categorization of endpoints within a large system. They can also facilitate searching and reporting on endpoints based on specific criteria or attributes, streamlining operations and maintenance tasks.

Define the deployment

When deploying a model to Azure Machine Learning, it's essential to begin by preparing the necessary components: model files, scoring script, and the computing environment. Model files are the trained machine learning models ready for deployment. The scoring script is crucial because it contains the code to invoke the model and process input data to generate predictions. Finally, the environment must be set up correctly, involving a Docker image and a set of Conda dependencies that ensure all necessary libraries and tools are available to run the model.

Once these elements are prepared, the next step is to configure the deployment settings. This includes specifying the model path where the model files are stored and detailing the code configuration through the scoring script. Additionally, the deployment's computing environment must be explicitly defined, including the Docker image and Conda dependencies. These settings play a role in ensuring that the model runs in an environment that replicates the one it was trained in, thereby reducing the likelihood of runtime errors.

A Docker image encapsulates the environment in which your machine learning model will run. This includes everything from the operating system, libraries, and dependencies required to run the model, ensuring consistency across different environments (e.g., from development to production). This isolation is crucial for avoiding conflicts between different software versions and making the deployment process more reliable.

Most often, the Docker image used in machine learning deployments is based on a standard Linux distribution, such as Ubuntu. The key component within this image is the Conda environment, which is defined by a conda.yaml file. This file specifies the necessary Python packages and their versions, ensuring that the correct dependencies are installed within the Docker container. A simple example follows:

```
$schema: https://azuremlschemas.azureedge.net/latest/managedOnlineDeployment.schema.json
name: simple-deployment
endpoint_name: my-endpoint
model:
  path: ./model/
```

```
code_configuration:
  code: ./scoring/
  scoring_script: score.py
environment:
  conda_file: ./environment/conda.yaml
  image: mcr.microsoft.com/azureml/openmpi4.1.0-ubuntu20.04:latest
instance_type: Standard_DS2_v2
instance_count: 1
```

Imagine a scenario where a tech company needs to deploy a machine learning model to predict user engagement based on app usage patterns. They prepare the model and scoring script based on historical data and configure a robust environment with Docker and Conda to handle dependencies. For deployment, they choose GPU-based instances due to the model's complexity and set the instance count to five to handle high-traffic volumes efficiently. This setup ensures that the model delivers real-time predictions accurately and efficiently, enhancing the user experience by providing personalized content and recommendations.

Deploy the model locally (optional)

Creating a local endpoint using the Azure command-line interface (CLI) is an effective method for testing and debugging machine learning models before deploying them to a production environment. This process starts with setting up the necessary environment and configurations specific to your model in the Azure environment. By using the Azure CLI, you can streamline the deployment of your model by creating a local endpoint directly from your development machine. This allows you to mimic the behavior of your model under a managed environment, providing a sandbox for safe testing and debugging. Commands in the Azure CLI can be used to configure the model, set up the endpoint specifications, and deploy the model without needing to interact with the Azure portal manually.

Once the local endpoint is set up, it's crucial to verify that the deployment has been successful. This can be accomplished by checking the provisioning state of the deployment through the Azure CLI. The provisioning state provides information about the status of the deployment, whether it's still in progress or has succeeded or failed. This step ensures that the model is properly instantiated and ready for testing. Furthermore, you can invoke the endpoint to score data, which involves sending requests to the endpoint with sample data and evaluating the responses. This test is vital because it not only checks the operational status of the model but also verifies that the model's outputs are as expected based on the input data provided.

Testing locally with the Azure CLI not only helps in identifying any issues in the early stages of the deployment process but also significantly reduces the complexity and cost associated with deploying models directly in a live environment. By iteratively testing and debugging through local endpoints, you can ensure that the model performs accurately and reliably before scaling up to a full production deployment. This practice is crucial for maintaining the integrity and efficiency of machine learning operations, allowing developers to fine-tune applications based on real feedback and performance metrics without disrupting ongoing operations. Once fully validated and optimized, the model can then be confidently rolled out to production with a higher assurance of success.

Deploy the model to Azure

Deploying a model to Azure involves several key steps to ensure the model is operational and can handle real-time data scoring efficiently. To begin, you use the Azure command-line interface (CLI) to create an endpoint and a deployment for your model. This process is crucial as it sets up the infrastructure required for your model to receive and process requests.

Here's a simplified command sequence to create an endpoint and a deployment in Azure.

CREATE THE ENDPOINT

The first step before creating an endpoint is to configure a name for your endpoint. In this example, we use the placeholder YOUR_ENDPOINT_NAME. You also need to specify a YAML file for your endpoint.

```
az ml online-endpoint create --name YOUR_ENDPOINT_NAME -f endpoint.yml
```

This command initializes the endpoint configuration from a YAML file (endpoint.yml), which specifies the endpoint's properties. The next step is to create the deployment; a code snippet is shown:

```
az ml online-deployment create --name YOUR_DEPLOYMENT_NAME --endpoint YOUR_ENDPOINT_NAME
-f deployment.yml --all-traffic
```

This command sets up the deployment using another YAML file (deployment.yml), directing all traffic to this new deployment, which is particularly useful during testing phases.

Once the deployment is active, it's crucial to monitor its status and check the logs for any potential errors. This ensures that the deployment is functioning correctly and is ready to process incoming data requests. You can check the deployment status and fetch logs using these commands:

```
az ml online-endpoint show -n YOUR_ENDPOINT_NAME
az ml online-deployment get-logs --name YOUR_DEPLOYMENT_NAME --endpoint
YOUR_ENDPOINT_NAME
```

It is a good practice to test the model's performance by invoking the endpoint using the Azure CLI or a REST client like curl:

```
az ml online-endpoint invoke --name YOUR_ENDPOINT_NAME --request-file sample-request.json
```

Optionally, you can enhance your deployment by updating components such as the scoring script. This might involve changing the logic within the script to improve performance or accuracy, and then redeploying using the updated YAML configuration. Autoscaling can also be configured to dynamically adjust the number of VM instances based on the workload, ensuring efficient resource use during varying levels of demand. Autoscaling settings can be specified in the deployment YAML or managed through the Azure portal to maintain optimal performance without manual intervention.

Monitor SLA and integrate with log analytics (optional)

Monitoring the service-level agreement (SLA) is an essential practice in ensuring that Azure Machine Learning deployments perform according to set standards. Using Azure Monitor, you can continuously oversee the performance metrics that relate directly to the SLA criteria. This real-time monitoring helps quickly identify and address service disruptions or degradations that could affect user experience or system reliability. By setting up proactive alerts, stakeholders are immediately notified if the SLA parameters are breached, allowing for swift remedial actions to restore service quality.

For enhanced log management, integrating with Log Analytics provides a robust solution for storing, analyzing, and querying extensive logs generated by Azure services. This integration allows teams to perform detailed diagnostics and retrospectively analyze data for insights, which is invaluable for troubleshooting, compliance, and optimizing system performance. Through Log Analytics, users gain access to advanced analytics tools and dashboards that can highlight trends and potential anomalies over time, supporting a data-driven approach to operational excellence.

Table 4-4 summarizes key actions and their benefits in monitoring SLAs and integrating with Log Analytics, providing a clear framework for Azure users to ensure their deployments are not only robust but also aligned with best practices for cloud management and operations.

TABLE 4-4 Summary of monitoring SLA and Log Analytics integration

Action	Tool Used	Purpose	Benefits
Monitor SLA	Azure Monitor	Ensure deployment meets performance standards of SLA	Quick identification and resolution of performance issues
Set Alerts for SLA Breach	Azure Monitor	Notify stakeholders of any deviations from SLA standards	Proactive management and minimization of downtime
Integrate with Log Analytics	Log Analytics	Store and analyze logs for a long-term	Enhanced troubleshooting, compliance, and operational insights

Delete the endpoint and deployment

If the deployment is no longer needed, delete the endpoint and its underlying deployments to free up resources. When managing cloud resources in Azure Machine Learning, it is essential to decommission online endpoints and their deployments when they are no longer in use. This step is vital to prevent unnecessary costs and free up resources. The Azure command-line interface (CLI) provides a simple and effective method to delete these components, ensuring all related resources are also terminated. This action helps avoid any lingering resource usage that could incur additional expenses.

At some point in the lifecycle of the endpoint, you may need to delete an online endpoint along with its deployments when it is no longer used. You can use the following Azure CLI command; however, this is a destructive operation:

```
az ml online-endpoint delete --name YOUR_ENDPOINT_NAME --yes --no-wait
```

This command prompts Azure to delete the specified endpoint and all its associated deployments immediately, without waiting for user confirmation (--yes) and without blocking the CLI (--no-wait). This ensures a fast, efficient cleanup of resources. The use of these flags is particularly useful in scripts or automated workflows where prompts or interactive inputs are undesirable.

> **NOTE DEPLOYING MODELS TO ONLINE ENDPOINTS**
>
> For further details on how to deploy models to online endpoints and manage them effectively throughout their lifecycle, including the deployment and decommissioning phases, Azure's comprehensive documentation (*https://learn.microsoft.com/en-us/azure/machine-learning/concept-endpoints-online*) offers step-by-step guides. These resources are invaluable for users looking to leverage Azure Machine Learning for robust, scalable machine learning deployments.

Deploy a model to a batch endpoint

Batch endpoints in Azure Machine Learning are used for deploying models to run inference over large volumes of data. They are ideal for scenarios where models require longer inference time, need to process large amounts of data, don't have low latency requirements, and can benefit from parallelization. Prerequisites include:

- Appropriate permissions in the workspace to create/manage batch endpoints and deployments.
- Azure CLI with ML extension installed.
- You should also create a compute cluster named batch-cluster with Azure Machine Learning compute or Kubernetes clusters.

Create a batch endpoint

In order to effectively use Azure Machine Learning for batch processing tasks, creating a compute cluster and configuring a batch endpoint are crucial steps. Before you can deploy your batch processing tasks, you must have a suitable compute resource. In Azure Machine Learning, batch jobs run on compute clusters that can dynamically scale according to the workload.

You can use the Azure CLI to create your compute cluster with the following command:

```
az ml compute create -n batch-cluster --type amlcompute --min-instances 0
--max-instances 5
```

This command sets up an Azure Machine Learning compute cluster named batch-cluster with a scaling range from 0 to 5 instances, making it efficient for variable batch processing loads.

Once your compute cluster is ready, you can configure and create a batch endpoint. This endpoint acts as the interface for batch processing jobs in Azure Machine Learning. Here are the steps to configure and create your batch endpoint:

1. Define a Unique Name: Establish a unique name for your batch endpoint. This name must be unique within the Azure region as it is used to construct the invocation URI. For example, you might name your endpoint hello-batch.

2. Prepare the Endpoint Configuration File: Create a YAML file, typically named endpoint. yml, which will specify the configuration of the batch endpoint. This file includes the endpoint's name, a description of the endpoint's purpose, and optional tags for easy identification and management. Below is an example of what the YAML configuration might look like:

```yaml
$schema: https://azuremlschemas.azureedge.net/latest/batchEndpoint.schema.json
name: hello-batch
description: A hello world endpoint for component deployments.
auth_mode: aad_token
```

This configuration sets the endpoint to use Azure Active Directory token-based authentication (aad_token), ensuring secure access.

With the YAML file prepared, we can finally use the Azure CLI to create the batch endpoint:

```
az ml batch-endpoint create --name hello-batch -f endpoint.yml
```

This command creates the batch endpoint using the specifications in the endpoint.yml file.

Create a batch deployment

Creating a batch deployment in Azure Machine Learning involves several key steps that allow you to operationalize your machine learning models efficiently for batch processing tasks. Below is a detailed description of each step based on official documentation:

Before deploying, the model you intend to use must be registered in your Azure Machine Learning workspace. This allows the model to be managed centrally and reused across various deployments. Here's how you can register your model (ensure that your model is ready and accessible before proceeding):

1. Register the Model: Use the Azure CLI or Python SDK to register the model to your workspace. For instance, using the Azure CLI: `az ml model register -n my-model-name -p path/to/model/file`.

2. Create a Scoring Script: The scoring script is crucial as it defines how the model will process input data to generate predictions. This script should include at least two functions:

   - Using `init()`: This function is called when the deployment starts. It is typically used for loading the model into a global object. This process ensures the model is loaded once per instance and reused for multiple scoring calls.

   - Using `run(raw_data)`: This function is called each time a batch job is run. It processes the input data, applies the model, and returns the results.

The environment specifies the dependencies required by your model. It includes any libraries or frameworks your model needs to function correctly. You can define this environment using a Conda environment file or directly within a Docker image by using an Azure ML base image. Here's an example of defining an environment using a Conda YAML file:

```yaml
name: myenv
dependencies:
  - python=3.8
  - scikit-learn
  - pip:
    - azureml-defaults
```

Register this environment to your Azure Machine Learning workspace:

```
az ml environment create -f path/to/conda_env.yml
```

The deployment configuration is defined in a YAML file. This file includes the model, code configuration, environment, compute target, and other settings. Here's an example of what this YAML might look like:

```yaml
$schema: https://azuremlschemas.azureedge.net/latest/batchDeployment.schema.json
name: my-batch-deployment
endpoint_name: my-batch-endpoint
model: azureml:my-model:1
environment: azureml:my-env:1
code_configuration:
  code: path/to/scoring/script
  scoring_script: score.py
compute: azureml:batch-cluster
resources:
  instance_count: 1
```

Finally, create the batch deployment under the batch endpoint using the Azure CLI, referencing the YAML configuration file:

```
az ml batch-deployment create -f deployment.yml --endpoint my-batch-endpoint
--set-default
```

The `--set-default` flag is optional and sets this deployment as the default for the endpoint.

Run batch endpoints and access results

In order to invoke a batch endpoint for triggering a batch scoring job in Azure Machine Learning, you specify the path to the input data, which is crucial for processing. The invocation is typically done via the Azure CLI or through the Python SDK, where you use the specific endpoint name and the data details. The input data path must be accurately specified to ensure that the model processes the correct data. This step initiates the scoring process where the model applies its predictive logic to the input data batch. This process is vital for generating results that will drive business decisions or further data analysis.

Monitoring the execution progress of the batch job is essential to ensure that it runs smoothly and efficiently. Azure Machine Learning provides tools to track the status and health of the job, with the ability to stream logs in real time using the Azure CLI command `az ml job stream`. After the job completes, the scoring results are typically stored in Azure cloud storage, such as an Azure Blob Storage container. If necessary, you can configure the output location for these results through the batch deployment's YAML configuration, specifying the desired storage account and container. This setup not only allows for organized data management but also facilitates easy access and analysis of the output data, enabling timely insights and actions based on the model's predictions.

Add deployments to an endpoint

Adding deployments to an existing endpoint is a strategic approach in managing machine learning models that allows for the simultaneous running of multiple versions or types under a single endpoint. This setup is particularly advantageous for comparing the performance of different models under identical environmental conditions without interrupting the current services. By utilizing deployment configurations, data scientists can test variations of models to determine which performs best before making a full-scale rollout. The process involves preparing a deployment configuration file, typically in YAML format, which details the model to be used, the runtime environment, and various parameters that govern the deployment.

Once the deployment configuration is finalized, deploying it to an existing endpoint is straightforward using the Azure command-line interface (CLI). The specific command used might look something like this:

```
az ml batch-deployment create --name <deployment-name> --endpoint <endpoint-name> --file
<config-file.yaml>
```

This command precisely directs the deployment to add under the specified endpoint. This command links the new deployment with the existing endpoint by referencing the configuration file. This flexibility is critical for managing lifecycle versions of machine learning models, allowing seamless updates and iterations without any downtime or disruption to the endpoint's ongoing operations.

This method of adding deployments fosters an environment of continuous improvement and testing within machine learning projects. It offers the opportunity to:

- **Experiment** Quickly test and compare different models or model versions in a controlled environment.

- **Roll Out Changes Gradually** Introduce changes incrementally to monitor impact and performance, reducing risks.

- **Maintain Service Continuity** Keep the existing model running without interruption as new models are deployed and tested.

EXAM TIP

When preparing for an exam on Azure Machine Learning services, remember that under-standing the commands and configurations necessary for managing deployments via the Azure CLI is crucial. Focus on mastering how to create, update, and manage different deployment configurations effectively, as this is often a key component of operational tasks in a real-world Azure environment.

Delete the batch endpoint and deployment

When a deployment or an entire endpoint is no longer needed, deleting them helps man-age costs and resource usage efficiently. To delete a specific deployment, you use the Azure CLI command `az ml batch-deployment delete`, specifying the name of the endpoint and the deployment. This action removes the particular deployment but leaves the endpoint and any other deployments intact. If you need to remove the entire endpoint, which includes all its underlying deployments, the command `az ml batch-endpoint delete` is used. This command should be executed with caution as it frees up all resources associated with the endpoint but also removes all deployments linked to it. Proper management of deployments and endpoints ensures that resources are allocated efficiently and that only necessary services consume cloud resources.

These tasks highlight the operational flexibility and resource management capabilities within Azure Machine Learning, allowing users to optimize their environments according to their project's lifecycle and resource requirements.

Test an online deployed service

Deploying machine learning models as online endpoints in Azure Machine Learning requires meticulous attention to ensure they operate correctly. Before considering a deployment successful, thorough testing and troubleshooting are imperative. This ensures that the model responds as expected to requests and performs accurately under various conditions. Testing involves simulating real-world traffic to the endpoint to verify its responsiveness and the correctness of its outputs. Troubleshooting, on the other hand, focuses on identifying and resolving issues that arise during these tests, such as performance bottlenecks, incorrect model outputs, or configuration errors in the deployment setup.

The process begins by setting up test scenarios that closely mimic the expected real-world use of the model. This might include a variety of inputs to test the model's robustness and edge cases that could potentially lead to failures. Monitoring tools and logs provided by Azure Machine Learning can be invaluable during this phase, as they provide detailed insights into the endpoint's performance and behavior. Common issues that might be identified during testing include slow response times, unexpected downtime, or incorrect data processing, which can then be addressed before the endpoint is released for live traffic.

This systematic approach to deploying machine learning models in Azure involves a few key strategies:

- **Regular Monitoring** Keep an eye on the endpoint's health and performance metrics using Azure's monitoring tools.
- **Load Testing** Simulate different loads to ensure that the model can handle expected and peak traffic.
- **Error Handling** Implement robust error handling in the deployment to manage unexpected input and operational errors gracefully.

Knowing how to effectively test and debug online endpoints not only ensures a smooth operational model but also mitigates potential risks in deployment, making it a vital skill set for real-world applications.

Deploy locally for testing

Before deploying your model to the cloud, it's recommended to deploy it locally to test and debug any issues. This can be done using a local Docker environment, which simulates cloud deployment. Using the Azure Machine Learning inference HTTP server package simulates the environment of an Azure endpoint and provides a way to validate the script's functionality:

```
az ml online-deployment create --endpoint-name <endpoint-name> -n <deployment-name> -f
<spec_file.yaml> --local
```

Test the scoring script

Ensuring the functionality of the scoring script, typically named score.py, is a critical step when deploying machine learning models in Azure Machine Learning. This script is important for processing incoming data and returning predictions. It generally includes two main functions: `init()` for initializing the model or loading necessary resources and `run()` for processing the input data to generate and return predictions. Testing the scoring script is crucial before deployment to avoid errors and ensure that it handles inputs as expected. This can be achieved by running the script locally using the Azure Machine Learning inference HTTP server package, which simulates the environment of an Azure endpoint and provides a straightforward way to validate the script's functionality.

During deployment, issues such as execution errors, performance bottlenecks, or unexpected behavior can arise. In such cases, container logs are invaluable for diagnosing problems. These logs capture detailed information about the operations of the deployment, including errors and system messages that can help pinpoint the source of a problem. To access these logs, you can use the Azure CLI command:

```
az ml online-deployment get-logs -e <endpoint-name> -n <deployment-name> -l 100
```

This command retrieves the last 100 lines of logs from the specified deployment, providing immediate insights into recent activities and issues.

Here are key strategies to ensure effective deployment and troubleshooting:

- **Test Locally** Always test the score.py script in a local environment to catch and fix issues early.
- **Log Analysis** Regularly review deployment logs to understand the behavior of the deployment and quickly identify anomalies or errors.
- **Incremental Deployment** Roll out changes in stages to monitor the impact and ensure stability before full deployment.

Invoke the batch endpoint to start a batch scoring job

Deploying and testing a model in Azure Machine Learning (Azure ML) is a critical phase in the machine learning lifecycle, ensuring that the model performs as expected in a live environment. Once a model is deployed to an endpoint, the immediate next step is to validate its functionality. This testing is typically conducted by sending sample requests using tools like curl or Postman, which simulate how real applications will interact with the model. It is crucial during these tests to use the correct authentication headers and payload format to mimic actual operational conditions accurately.

Azure ML provides robust monitoring capabilities that are essential for maintaining the health and performance of your deployed models. Through integration with Azure Monitor, you can track vital metrics such as request rate, response time, and error rate. Monitoring these metrics helps identify performance bottlenecks and ensures that the model meets the required service level agreements and performance benchmarks. This continuous monitoring is fundamental for proactive management of the machine learning model in production.

Furthermore, utilizing HTTP status codes for debugging can provide immediate insights into the nature of any issues encountered when the model endpoint is invoked. A 200 status code indicates a successful request, while codes like 401 (authentication error) or 500 (internal server error) pinpoint specific areas that require attention. Understanding these codes and the associated error messages can significantly expedite the troubleshooting process, helping maintain the reliability and efficiency of machine learning operations in Azure. By mastering these steps and strategies, users can ensure that their deployed models are not only operational but also optimized for performance and stability in a production environment.

Once deployed, test the endpoint by sending a sample request. This can be done using tools like curl or Postman. Ensure that you include the correct authentication headers and payload format. You'll need to manage key rotation regularly and understand that the Authorization header usually contains either a long-lived key or a short-lived bearer token that needs periodic refreshing.

Azure Machine Learning provides monitoring capabilities through Azure Monitor. Check metrics like request rate, response time, and error rate to ensure that your endpoint is performing as expected.

Troubleshoot common errors

When you deploy models in Azure Machine Learning, you may encounter errors that can interrupt the deployment process. Understanding these common errors and knowing how to troubleshoot them is a necessary skill for ensuring smooth deployments. Below are some typical issues you might face, along with tips on how to resolve them:

- **ImageBuildFailure**   Check the build log for details. Ensure that the environment specifications in the conda.yaml file are correct.
- **OutOfQuota**   Verify that you have sufficient quota for the resources required by your deployment.
- **BadArgument**   Ensure that all specifications in your deployment configuration are correct and that resources like models and environments are properly registered.
- **ResourceNotReady**   Check if the container is crashing due to errors in the scoring script or environment setup.
- **ResourceNotFound**   Verify that all specified resources, such as models and storage accounts, exist and are accessible.
- **OperationCanceled**   This may occur if there is a higher priority operation in progress. Retry the operation after some time.
- **InternalServerError**   Indicates an issue with the Azure Machine Learning service. Contact Azure support for assistance.
- Use HTTP Status Codes for Debugging

Skill 4.2: Apply machine learning operations (MLOps) practices

Applying machine learning operations (MLOps) practices within Azure Machine Learning is crucial for streamlining the deployment, maintenance, and scalability of machine learning models. MLOps is a set of practices that combines machine learning, DevOps, and data engineering, and aims to deploy and maintain ML systems in production reliably and efficiently. The ability to automate the machine learning lifecycle enables businesses to accelerate their ML initiatives and achieve higher efficiency and consistency in operations.

Azure Machine Learning provides a robust framework for implementing MLOps practices, facilitating continuous integration, continuous delivery, and continuous training (CI/CD/CT) of machine learning models. The platform supports various tools and pipelines that allow data scientists and ML engineers to automate the workflow of machine learning models from development to production. This includes version control of data and models, automated testing, and monitoring of models in production to ensure performance and accuracy remain high. The integration of these tools into a cohesive pipeline reduces manual errors and improves the reproducibility of machine learning experiments.

One key aspect of implementing MLOps in Azure is the use of Azure Pipelines. Azure Pipelines is a CI/CD service that supports automatic model training and testing, environment management, and deployment of ML models to various production environments. This ensures that models are always tested, integrated, and delivered systematically, reducing the chances of errors and downtime in production systems. Additionally, Azure Machine Learning's ability to track experiments and manage resources allows teams to optimize their operations and streamline the management of machine learning projects.

Monitoring and maintaining model performance over time is another critical component of MLOps. Azure Machine Learning provides tools to monitor the health and performance of models continuously. It tracks metrics such as accuracy, prediction time, and resource utilization, triggering alerts when a model's performance degrades or deviates from expected patterns. This proactive monitoring enables teams to quickly identify and rectify issues, possibly automating the retraining and redeployment of models using pipelines when necessary.

To better understand an MLOps pipeline in Azure Machine Learning, consider the key components shown in Table 4-5.

TABLE 4-5 Key components of an MLOps pipeline in Azure Machine Learning

Component	Description
Version Control	Manages and stores versions of models and data
Continuous Integration	Automates the testing and building of ML models
Continuous Delivery	Automates the deployment of ML models to production
Continuous Training	Automates retraining of models with new data
Monitoring	Tracks performance metrics and health of deployed models
Experiment Tracking	Logs experiments to ensure reproducibility

A pipeline has additional considerations around scalability, types of operations (training, deployment, validation), and security.

- **Automated Workflows** Implement automated pipelines for training, validation, and deployment to streamline operations.
- **Scalability** Utilize Azure's global infrastructure to scale machine learning workflows as needed.
- **Security and Compliance** Ensure that data and models comply with organizational and regulatory standards.

When preparing for an Azure certification that includes machine learning, focus on understanding how MLOps practices can be implemented using Azure Machine Learning. Familiarize yourself with the setup and management of pipelines, as well as the monitoring and maintenance of models in a production environment. This knowledge is crucial for effectively managing machine learning workflows and ensuring that models remain accurate and performant over time.

Trigger an Azure Machine Learning job, including from Azure DevOps or GitHub

In the fast-paced world of data science and machine learning, maintaining the accuracy and relevance of models is important as data continuously evolves. Consider a scenario where a financial institution relies on predictive models to assess credit risk. Over time, economic conditions change, consumer behavior shifts, and the data underlying these models can drift significantly from the state when the models were initially trained. This drift can degrade the model's accuracy, leading to suboptimal decision-making. To manage this, Azure Machine Learning provides robust tools to detect and respond to changes in the model's training data automatically.

Another illustrative scenario involves a healthcare organization using machine learning models to predict patient outcomes based on clinical data. As new treatment methods are introduced and demographic shifts occur, the original datasets used to train these models may no longer reflect current trends. By implementing dataset monitoring and automated retraining workflows, the organization can ensure that their models adapt to new data, maintaining their efficacy in predicting patient outcomes accurately.

Retail businesses can also benefit from these technologies, especially in dynamic environments like fashion and consumer electronics, where customer preferences and market conditions can change rapidly. By setting up Azure Machine Learning dataset monitors, retailers can detect shifts in customer buying patterns and adjust their inventory and marketing strategies accordingly. One scenario where monitoring can be used is to monitor the real choice made by the customer and the prediction: when the prediction and choice made by the customer diverge too much, the model should be retrained. This proactive approach allows businesses to stay ahead of trends and manage their operations more effectively, ensuring that they meet the evolving needs of their customers.

Both Azure DevOps and GitHub Actions can be used to automate the process of training and deploying machine learning models on Azure Machine Learning. This guide provides a general overview of setting up workflows in both platforms to trigger Azure Machine Learning jobs.

There are a few prerequisites for this section:

- An Azure Machine Learning workspace.
- A GitHub or Azure DevOps account, and a repository or project for your code.
- The Azure CLI with the ML extension installed.

Authentication and securely handling credentials

Saving and running the pipeline in an Azure Machine Learning context involves authenticating with Azure using a service principal. This authentication process enables the pipeline to trigger specified machine learning jobs as defined in the job.yml file. This step is crucial for ensuring that the pipeline has the necessary permissions to access and execute tasks within the Azure environment, effectively linking the automation setup with Azure's robust cloud capabilities.

Similarly, the setup process for GitHub Actions mirrors that of Azure DevOps. Start by creating a service principal through the Azure CLI. This action generates credentials that are critical for authenticating and authorizing operations in Azure. Once these credentials are obtained, the next step is to securely store them as secrets in your GitHub repository. Doing so ensures that sensitive information remains protected and that GitHub Actions can access Azure resources without exposing these credentials in the workflow configuration.

For both Azure DevOps and GitHub Actions, securely handling the service principal credentials involves storing them in the platform's secrets management system. However, Azure DevOps uses Azure Key Vault or the built-in Library to store secrets. You can link service connections and variable groups to your pipelines to securely access these secrets. This setup not only secures sensitive data but also allows scripts and pipelines to operate with enhanced security. By following these steps, developers can maintain a secure and efficient CI/CD pipeline that leverages Azure Machine Learning services, ensuring automated, scalable, and secure machine learning workflows. In the next sections, we will cover GitHub and Azure DevOps separately.

Automating Azure Machine Learning with Azure DevOps

In Azure DevOps, you can integrate your project with Azure resources by setting up a service connection, allowing secure interaction between your DevOps pipelines and your cloud infrastructure. Once the connection is configured, you can create and manage pipelines that automate the deployment and management of your applications.

CREATE A SERVICE CONNECTION

In Azure DevOps, navigate to a specific project and then choose a connection type. Go to Project Settings > Service Connections > New Service Connection.

Choose Azure Resource Manager and set up the connection with the appropriate subscription and resource group. You will also need a pipeline to work with by following the steps below to create a new one. I will reference this pipeline throughout the example:

1. Navigate to Pipelines > New Pipeline.
2. Connect to your code repository and select the Azure Repos Git or GitHub option.
3. Define your pipeline using YAML. An example azure-pipelines.yml might look like this:

```yaml
trigger:
- main
```

```
pool:
  vmImage: 'ubuntu-latest'

steps:
- script: |
    az login --service-principal -u $(clientId) -p $(clientSecret) --tenant
$(tenantId)
    az ml job create --file job.yml --resource-group $(resourceGroup) --workspace-
name $(workspaceName)
  displayName: 'Train model on Azure ML'
```

Replace the environmental variables with your Azure ML workspace details and the service principal credentials (`clientId`, `clientSecret`, and `tenantId`, which are necessary for authenticating with Azure services) that you collected in the prerequisites.

DEFINE VARIABLES

When setting up an Azure Machine Learning pipeline in GitHub Actions, you can use variables and configure pipeline variables correctly to ensure secure and efficient access to Azure services. This configuration should include service principal credentials—`clientId`, `clientSecret`, and `tenantId`—which are necessary for authenticating the Azure services. Additionally, variables such as `workspaceName` for the Azure Machine Learning workspace and `resourceGroup` for identifying the Azure resource group need to be established. These variables help streamline interactions with Azure resources during the pipeline's execution.

Integrating these variables into your GitHub Actions workflows involves defining them as secrets within the GitHub repository's settings under the Security tab. This approach ensures that sensitive information like service principal credentials is encrypted and safely accessed only within the GitHub Actions environment when needed. Storing secrets in this manner adheres to security best practices and protects your credentials from potential exposure.

By referencing these securely stored secrets in your GitHub Actions workflow files using the syntax `${{ secrets.VARIABLE_NAME }}`, you allow your workflow to dynamically use the necessary credentials and resource identifiers. This method maintains a high level of security and operational flexibility, facilitating safe and effective interactions with Azure Machine Learning services. This setup not only enhances the security but also simplifies the manageability of machine learning operations across various environments and deployment stages.

CONFIGURING SECRETS

Azure DevOps handles secrets using secure variables stored in variable groups or pipelines, where they are encrypted and masked in logs during execution. Secrets can be managed through the Azure Key Vault, ensuring they are not exposed directly in pipelines. This differs from GitHub Actions, where secrets are stored in the repository settings and are also masked during execution.

Automating Azure Machine Learning with GitHub

In this section, we will look at how to create a workflow with GitHub actions and will learn about some of the features available when working with actions. You can leverage what you learned in the previous section about Azure DevOps since, although there are differences, many of the concepts used for building CI pipelines remain the same, such as having a way to configure secrets.

CREATE A WORKFLOW WITH GITHUB ACTIONS

Both Azure DevOps and GitHub Actions offer robust capabilities for automating Azure Machine Learning jobs, simplifying the continuous integration and deployment (CI/CD) processes involved in machine learning projects. By leveraging these tools, teams can achieve more efficient workflows, faster iteration times, and more reliable deployments. Training and deploying machine learning models become systematic and controlled, reducing the likelihood of errors and inconsistencies. For further details and advanced configurations, one can explore the extensive documentation provided by Azure, such as the guide on using GitHub Actions for Azure Machine Learning, which offers deeper insights and more complex workflow examples.

Integrating GitHub Actions with Azure Machine Learning enhances the automation of machine learning workflows, making it easier to train and deploy models directly from your GitHub repository. To get started, you first need to set up a specific workflow file within your repository. This file, typically named something like ml-train.yml, should be located in the .github/workflows directory. This YAML file defines the steps your workflow will take each time it's triggered, ensuring that your machine learning training processes are executed automatically upon certain GitHub events, such as a push to the repository.

The structure of the workflow file in YAML format is straightforward yet powerful. For instance, consider a workflow named "Train ML Model" that triggers on push events. This setup utilizes GitHub Actions to handle the job execution on a virtual environment like ubuntu-latest. The workflow comprises several steps starting with checking out the code from the repository. Subsequent steps involve logging into Azure using the azure/login GitHub Action, which securely uses credentials stored as secrets in the GitHub repository. This is crucial for maintaining security and confidentiality of access keys.

Following authentication, the next step in the workflow is to execute a command to train a machine learning model on Azure ML. This is done by running a command line instruction that creates a job in Azure Machine Learning using a job definition file, such as job.yml. Here, resource group and workspace names are also pulled securely from GitHub secrets, showcasing the seamless integration of GitHub Actions with Azure's cloud services. This setup not only automates the training process but also ensures it is reproducible and consistent across different environments or even different teams.

In your GitHub repository, create a workflow file in the .github/workflows directory—for example, ml-train.yml.

Define your workflow using YAML. An example workflow might look like this:

```yaml
name: Train ML Model

on: [push]
```

```
jobs:
  train:
    runs-on: ubuntu-latest
    steps:
    - uses: actions/checkout@v2

    - name: Azure Login
      uses: azure/login@v1
      with:
        creds: ${{ secrets.AZURE_CREDENTIALS }}

    - name: Train model on Azure ML
      run: |
        az ml job create --file job.yml --resource-group ${{ secrets.RESOURCE_GROUP }}
--workspace-name ${{ secrets.WORKSPACE_NAME }}
```

The workflow will trigger on a push event to the repository. You can also manually trigger it or set it up to run on a schedule.

Configuring secrets in GitHub Actions for deploying Azure Machine Learning models is a critical step to ensure secure and efficient automation of machine learning workflows. GitHub Actions allows the automation of workflows, making it a powerful tool for implementing continuous integration and continuous delivery (CI/CD) practices in machine learning projects. By storing sensitive information such as Azure credentials in secrets, developers can manage and access these details securely without exposing them in the workflow scripts.

A service principal must be created using Azure CLI, which generates a JSON object containing credentials. This JSON object includes sensitive information such as `clientId`, `clientSecret`, `subscriptionId`, and `tenantId`. These credentials are necessary for GitHub Actions to authenticate with Azure and perform tasks such as training models, deploying them, or managing resources within the Azure Machine Learning workspace. The security of these operations hinges on the proper handling and storage of these credentials, ensuring they are not exposed in publicly accessible files or logs.

Once the service principal is created, the next step is to add these credentials to the GitHub repository as secrets. This can be done under the repository's settings, in the Security section, where you can add new secrets. These secrets are encrypted and only exposed to GitHub Actions runners during the execution of a workflow. By storing credentials as secrets, the workflow can use them to authenticate with Azure securely, without hard-coding sensitive information directly into the workflow files or exposing it to potential security risks.

Furthermore, in the GitHub Actions workflow file, these secrets are referenced using the syntax `${{ secrets.SECRET_NAME }}`, where `SECRET_NAME` would typically be `AZURE_CREDENTIALS`. This method of referencing ensures that the credentials are only used at runtime and remain secure. The workflow can include steps to authenticate with Azure using these credentials, set up the Azure Machine Learning CLI, and execute commands to train models or deploy them to production. Each step in the workflow can be configured to use Azure-specific actions, such as azure/login, which facilitates the login process using the provided Azure credentials from GitHub Secrets.

Overall, the use of GitHub Actions combined with Azure Machine Learning creates a robust framework for automating and managing machine learning deployments. By configuring secrets properly, teams can maintain a secure environment for CI/CD workflows that automate critical tasks like model training, validation, and deployment, ensuring that sensitive information is handled securely throughout the development and deployment process. Figure 4-2 illustrates this process.

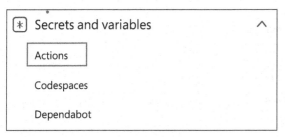

FIGURE 4-2 Secrets and variables in GitHub Actions

> ***NEED MORE REVIEW?*** **GITHUB ACTIONS FOR AZURE MACHINE LEARNING**
>
> You can read more about GitHub Actions for Azure Machine learning here: *https://learn.microsoft.com/en-us/azure/machine-learning/how-to-github-actions-machine-learning*

Both Azure DevOps and GitHub Actions provide robust platforms for automating Azure Machine Learning jobs. By integrating these CI/CD tools with Azure ML, you can streamline the process of training and deploying machine learning models, ensuring consistent and reproducible results.

Automate model retraining based on new data additions or data changes

When you need to automate model retraining based on data additions or changes, you can use Azure Machine Learning dataset monitors. These monitors can detect data drift, which is the change in model input data that can lead to model performance degradation. By setting up a dataset monitor, you can analyze drift in your data over time, monitor input data for differences between training and serving datasets, and set up alerts on data drift for early warnings. This allows you to create a new dataset version when the data has drifted too much, ensuring that your model remains accurate and up to date.

To add some assurance that your machine learning model remains accurate with changing data, you can set up an automated retraining pipeline in Azure Machine Learning. Here's how:

1. Create Datasets: Start by defining your baseline (training) and target (new data) datasets.

2. Set Up Data Drift Monitor: Create a data drift monitor to track changes in data distribution. Specify the datasets, features, and drift threshold.

3. Create Training Pipeline: Develop a pipeline for model training, including steps for preprocessing, training, and evaluation.

Table 4-6 shows various dataset monitor components and an example scenario for automating model retraining based on data changes.

TABLE 4-6 Dataset monitor components for retraining scenarios

Component	Description
Baseline Dataset	Usually the training dataset for a model.
Target Dataset	Data compared over time to the baseline dataset, typically model input data. Must have a timestamp.
Dataset Monitor	Detects and alerts to data drift, analyzes historical data, and profiles new data over time.
Drift Magnitude	Percentage indicating the drift between baseline and target datasets (0% = identical, 100% = completely different).
Drift Threshold	Set value beyond which an alert is triggered if the drift magnitude exceeds it.
Backfill Function	Runs a job for a specified date range to fill in expected missing data points in the dataset.

Finally, we can set up a monitoring system that automatically triggers the training pipeline when data drift exceeds a specified threshold. This can be achieved by using Azure Event Grid to detect the drift event and then using Azure Logic Apps or Azure Functions to initiate the pipeline in response to that event. This ensures that your model stays up-to-date and continues to perform well as data changes over time.

Deploy the pipeline and monitor for drift. The pipeline automatically retriggers when significant drift is detected. After retraining, evaluate and deploy the new model if it outperforms the old one. This setup ensures that your model adapts to changes in data, maintaining its accuracy over time.

> **NEED MORE REVIEW?** **AUTOMATING RETRAINING BASED ON NEW DATA**
>
> You can read about automating retraining based on new data additions or data changes here: *https://learn.microsoft.com/en-us/azure/machine-learning/how-to-monitor-datasets*

Define event-based retraining triggers

This section explains how to set up event-driven applications, processes, or CI/CD workflows that automatically respond to events in Azure Machine Learning using Azure Event Grid. This setup is essential for automating actions like sending notifications or triggering further ML pipeline runs when events like training completion, model registration, or data drift detection occur, making machine learning projects more efficient.

Azure Event Grid connects event sources, such as Azure Machine Learning, to event handlers like Azure Functions, Logic Apps, and Event Hubs. This allows for real-time processing of events, creating a responsive and dynamic environment for machine learning. This guide provides steps to set up and filter these events in the Azure portal, ensuring that only relevant events trigger specific workflows.

The setup process includes subscribing to events using the Azure portal, PowerShell, or Azure CLI, applying filters to control event flow, and selecting appropriate endpoints for event delivery. For example, you can filter events by run types or specific machine learning event types like model registration or run completion to streamline your workflows. The guide also highlights the importance of role-based access control (RBAC) to ensure that only authorized users can manage event subscriptions.

Practical uses of handling Azure Machine Learning events with Azure Event Grid include setting up email alerts for run completions or failures and integrating with Azure Logic Apps for more complex automations. The guide also offers tips for handling issues like event delivery failures or unexpected event types, helping users maintain a robust and automated machine learning lifecycle. A summary of available event types is provided in Table 4-7.

TABLE 4-7 Event types available in Azure Machine Learning

Event Type	Description
RunCompleted	Triggered when an experiment run completes
ModelRegistered	Triggered when a model is registered
ModelDeployed	Triggered when a model deployment completes
DatasetDriftDetected	Triggered when data drift is detected
RunStatusChanged	Triggered when a run's status changes

You can use these events to send notifications, trigger pipelines, or integrate with other services. Setting up event-driven workflows can be done through the Azure portal or CLI, providing a flexible and powerful way to automate and monitor your machine learning operations. Figure 4-3 shows a diagram of the machine learning lifecycle with model retraining.

NEED MORE REVIEW? **DEFINING EVENT-BASED RETRAINING TRIGGERS**

You can read more about defining event-based retraining triggers here: *https://learn.microsoft.com/en-us/azure/machine-learning/how-to-use-event-grid*

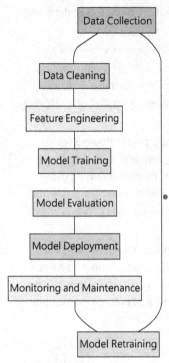

FIGURE 4-3 Machine learning lifecycle and model retraining

Best practices for each phase of the lifecycle

The lifecycle of machine learning operations (MLOps) in Azure Machine Learning is a comprehensive and iterative process that ensures the deployment of robust, scalable, and high-performing models. Note that MLOps lifecycle differs from the traditional ML lifecycle primarily in its focus on integrating machine learning with software development and operations practices. Each phase of this lifecycle is crucial for maintaining the integrity and efficiency of machine learning solutions. By following best practices at each stage, organizations can achieve reproducibility, scalability, and reliability in their machine learning workflows. Let's break down these phases and best practices in detail.

DATA COLLECTION AND INGESTION

In the initial phase, data collection and ingestion involve gathering raw data from various sources, including databases, APIs, and other data streams. This phase is critical as the quality of the input data directly affects the model's performance.

Best Practices:

- Ensure data quality and consistency by implementing data validation checks.
- Utilize Azure Data Factory for orchestrating complex data workflows and integrating various data sources.
- Implement data versioning to ensure reproducibility and track changes over time.

DATA CLEANING AND PREPARATION

Cleaning and preparing data involves removing inconsistencies, handling missing values, and correcting errors. The data is then transformed into a format suitable for analysis, which is crucial for accurate model training.

Here are some best practices for automating data cleaning:

- Automate data cleaning processes using Azure Databricks to handle large datasets efficiently.
- Manage and version data with Azure Machine Learning datasets to maintain a structured and organized workflow.
- Validate the cleaned data to ensure it meets quality standards before proceeding to the next phase.

FEATURE ENGINEERING

Feature engineering transforms raw data into meaningful features that can be used to train machine learning models. This phase is essential for enhancing the model's predictive power.

Best practices:

- Use automated feature engineering tools in Azure Machine Learning to streamline the process.
- Document all feature transformations to ensure reproducibility and transparency.
- Regularly update features to reflect changes in data patterns and maintain model accuracy.

MODEL TRAINING

Model training involves developing machine learning models using the prepared training data. This phase is where the actual learning happens, and it requires significant computational resources.

Best practices:

- Leverage Azure Machine Learning compute clusters for scalable and efficient model training.
- Optimize model performance through hyperparameter tuning.
- Track experiments and maintain detailed logs in Azure Machine Learning to ensure reproducibility and facilitate comparisons.

MODEL EVALUATION

Model evaluation assesses the performance of the trained model using validation data. It ensures that the model meets the desired accuracy and performance metrics before deployment.

Best practices:

- Use metrics and visualizations in Azure Machine Learning to thoroughly evaluate model performance.
- Implement cross-validation techniques to ensure the robustness of the model.
- Compare multiple models to select the best-performing one for deployment.

MODEL DEPLOYMENT

Deploying the trained model to a production environment allows it to make predictions on new data. This phase involves setting up infrastructure to support the model's operational requirements.

Best practices:

- Deploy models as web services using Azure Kubernetes Service (AKS) or Azure Container Instances (ACI) for scalability.
- Utilize Azure Machine Learning endpoints for seamless integration with other applications.
- Implement continuous integration and deployment (CI/CD) pipelines with Azure DevOps to automate the deployment process and ensure consistency.

MONITORING AND MAINTENANCE

Continuous monitoring and maintenance of the model's performance are crucial for maintaining its accuracy and reliability in a production environment. This phase ensures that the model adapts to changes in data patterns over time.

Best practices:

- Use Azure Monitor and Application Insights to track model performance metrics and log anomalies.
- Set up alerts to detect and respond to performance degradation promptly.
- Regularly retrain models with new data to address data drift and ensure ongoing accuracy.

MODEL RETRAINING

Model retraining involves updating the model with new data to improve its performance and adapt to evolving data patterns. This phase is essential for keeping the model relevant and accurate over time. Table 4-8 summarizes some of these best practices.

TABLE 4-8 Best practices for MLOps

Phase	Description	Best Practices
Data Collection and Ingestion	Gathering raw data from various sources.	Ensure data quality and consistency. Use Azure Data Factory for orchestrating data workflows. Implement data versioning for reproducibility.
Data Cleaning and Preparation	Cleaning the data to remove inconsistencies and preparing it for analysis.	Automate data cleaning processes with Azure Databricks. Use Azure Machine Learning datasets for managing and versioning data. Validate data quality.

Phase	Description	Best Practices
Feature Engineering	Transforming raw data into meaningful features for model training.	Use automated feature engineering tools in Azure Machine Learning Document feature transformations. Regularly update features to reflect data changes.
Model Training	Developing machine learning models using training data.	Leverage Azure Machine Learning compute clusters. Optimize model performance with hyperparameter tuning. Track experiments for reproducibility.
Model Evaluation	Assessing the model's performance using validation data.	Use Azure Machine Learning metrics and visualizations. Implement cross-validation. Compare multiple models to select the best-performing one.
Model Deployment	Deploying the trained model to a production environment.	Deploy models as web services using AKS or ACI. Use Azure Machine Learning endpoints. Implement CI/CD pipelines with Azure DevOps.
Monitoring and Maintenance	Continuously monitoring and maintaining the model's performance.	Use Azure Monitor and Application Insights. Set up alerts for performance degradation. Regularly retrain models with new data.
Model Retraining	Updating the model with new data to maintain performance and adapt to changes.	Automate retraining processes using Azure Machine Learning pipelines. Implement version control for models. Use AutoML for rapid retraining.

By adopting these best practices and leveraging the comprehensive suite of tools provided by Azure Machine Learning, organizations can ensure that their machine learning models are not only high-performing but also robust, scalable, and maintainable. MLOps provides the necessary framework to manage the entire lifecycle of machine learning models, from data collection and preparation to deployment and ongoing maintenance, ensuring that models continue to deliver value in real-world scenarios.

Table 4-8 summarizes some of the best practices we discussed and encapsulates the critical phases of the MLOps lifecycle and their corresponding best practices, providing a concise reference for ensuring effective machine learning operations within Azure Machine Learning.

Emerging trends in MLOps architectures

There are several technologies and patterns that are emerging in MLOps technologies like Microsoft Fabric, RAG, and context-aware MLOps that will impact how data science solutions are designed in the future. We will cover only a few of these trends (context-aware MLOps, Microsoft Fabric, and RAG, as well as Pareto decision boundaries) so you are familiar with terms like RAG as they come up in practice, but these will not be covered on the exam.

Microsoft Fabric is a unified data analytics platform that integrates various data services, including data engineering, data integration, data warehousing, data science, real-time analytics, and business intelligence. It simplifies and accelerates the process of building, managing, and deploying data-driven applications and solutions by providing a cohesive environment for efficient data management and analysis.

Context-aware MLOps with Microsoft Fabric and RAG

Building on the foundation provided by Microsoft Fabric, context-aware MLOps incorporates contextual information into the machine learning lifecycle to enhance model relevance and accuracy. Retrieval-augmented generation (RAG) can further enhance this process by dynamically integrating external data sources into model generation, ensuring that responses are both contextually relevant and up to date. Key Components of context-aware MLOps include:

1. **Data Ingestion and Processing**
   - Contextual Data Sources: Integrate diverse data sources, such as user behavior logs, environmental sensors, and external databases.
   - Dynamic Data Pipelines: Design adaptable data pipelines within Microsoft Fabric to ensure the most relevant data is available for model training and inference.
   - RAG Integration: Use RAG to dynamically retrieve and incorporate the latest information from external data sources during model inference. Legal professionals use RAG to quickly pull relevant case laws, statutes, or legal writings, streamlining the research process and ensuring that they have access to the most current legal information

2. **Model Training and Fine-Tuning**
   - Contextual Features: Incorporate contextual features into training data using Fabric's robust data engineering tools.
   - Real-Time Updates: Continuously update models with new contextual data through Fabric's real-time analytics capabilities.

3. **Model Deployment**
   - Adaptive Deployment: Deploy models that adjust their behavior based on the current context, utilizing Fabric's integration with edge computing for low-latency responses.
   - Edge Deployment: Implement edge computing within Fabric to bring context-aware models closer to the data source.

4. **Monitoring and Maintenance**
   - Contextual Monitoring: Use Fabric's monitoring systems to track contextual changes and their impact on model performance.

Visualizing Pareto tradeoffs in MLOps with Azure Machine Learning

As we transition from RAG (retrieval-augmented generation) to understanding broader optimization challenges in MLOps, we need to address how Pareto trade-offs help balance conflicting objectives like model accuracy, computational cost, and deployment latency. These trade-offs can be effectively visualized using well-established tools like Parallel Coordinate Plots (PCPs), enabling more informed decision-making across the ML lifecycle.

Visualizing Pareto trade-offs helps optimize multiple conflicting objectives, such as model accuracy, computational cost, and deployment latency. Azure Machine Learning provides tools for creating specific visualizations to analyze these trade-offs. One effective visualization technique is the Parallel Coordinate Plot (PCP), which can be augmented for use in MLOps and is a useful way to visualize the many trade-offs data scientists make when monitoring machine learning solutions. Here are a few to explore further:

- **Dynamic Exploration**   Implement interactive PCPs to allow MLOps practitioners to dynamically explore high-dimensional data related to model performance, hyperparameters, and other relevant metrics.

- **Enhanced Interpretability**   Use color schemes to represent different model versions, datasets, or experiment runs, enhancing the interpretability of PCPs in an MLOps context.

- **Pattern Identification**   Incorporate brushing and linking functionality to enable users to select specific ranges of values across multiple axes, facilitating the identification of patterns and relationships between different MLOps metrics.

- **Uncover Hidden Patterns**   Allow dynamic reordering of axes to help uncover hidden patterns and correlations between different MLOps parameters and performance metrics.

- **Unified View**   Embed PCPs into existing MLOps dashboards or platforms to provide a unified view of model performance, data drift, and other relevant metrics across the ML lifecycle.

You can try augmenting PCPs with these features, and MLOps teams can gain deeper insights into model behavior, performance trade-offs, and the impact of various parameters on model outcomes.

Here's an example of how to create an interactive PCP using Plotly in Python:

```
import plotly.express as px
import pandas as pd

# Example data
data = pd.DataFrame({
    'Model': ['Model A', 'Model B', 'Model C', 'Model D'],
    'Accuracy': [0.85, 0.88, 0.90, 0.87],
    'Computational Cost': [200, 500, 800, 300],
    'Deployment Latency (ms)': [50, 80, 60, 100],
    'Parameters (Millions)': [10, 20, 15, 30]
})

# Creating a parallel coordinates plot
fig = px.parallel_coordinates(data, color='Accuracy',
                              dimensions=['Computational Cost', 'Deployment Latency
(ms)', 'Parameters (Millions)'],
                              color_continuous_scale=px.colors.diverging.Tealrose,
                              color_continuous_midpoint=0.88)
```

```
fig.update_layout(
    title="Parallel Coordinate Plot for MLOps Trade-offs",
    coloraxis_colorbar=dict(
        title="Accuracy",
        tickvals=[0.85, 0.88, 0.90],
        ticktext=["0.85", "0.88", "0.90"]
    )
)

fig.show()
```

Azure Machine Learning can facilitate the implementation of these visualizations as part of a comprehensive data science solution. Figure 4-4 shows an example of the PCP plot.

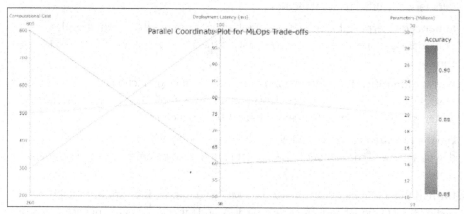

FIGURE 4-4 Parallel coordinate plot for visualizing MLOps trade-offs

We've discussed some advanced topics in this section, like integrating Microsoft Fabric with Azure Machine Learning for context-aware MLOps and visualizing Pareto trade-offs through augmented Parallel Coordinate Plots. Utilizing RAG further enhances model relevance and accuracy by dynamically incorporating external data. These visualizations enable MLOps practitioners to dynamically explore and understand the complex relationships between different metrics, optimizing resource allocation, improving model performance, and ensuring adaptive, contextually relevant models in dynamic environments.

Chapter summary

- You can configure settings for online deployment, customizing the environment to ensure optimal performance and scalability.
- You can now configure compute resources specifically for batch deployments, aligning processing power with the data volume and computational needs of the task.
- You can deploy a model to an online endpoint, providing real-time predictive services accessible via an API.

- You can now deploy a model to a batch endpoint, enabling scheduled or on-demand processing of large data sets.

- You can test an online deployed service to verify its functionality and performance under real-world operating conditions.

- You can now invoke the batch endpoint to start a batch scoring job, processing data efficiently in a non-interactive manner.

- Users can build a pipeline and run it once a push is made, including from Azure DevOps or GitHub, integrating MLOps practices into existing CI/CD pipelines.

- You can now automate model retraining based on new data additions or changes, ensuring that the model remains accurate over time.

- You can define event-based retraining triggers, creating a responsive and adaptive machine learning system.

- You learned that emerging technologies and architectural patterns like RAG architecture and Microsoft Fabric may impact how data science and machine learning solutions are designed in Microsoft Azure.

Thought experiment

In this thought experiment, demonstrate your skills and knowledge of the topics covered in this chapter. You can find the answers in the section that follows.

1. Online Model Deployment: How can users ensure their online deployed models perform optimally?

   A. Deploy without testing the model's response time.

   B. Configure settings for online deployment tailored to the model's requirements.

   C. Use default settings regardless of specific model needs.

   D. Limit access to the deployed model to reduce load.

2. Batch Deployment Strategy: What is critical when configuring the compute for a batch deployment?

   A. Assign minimal compute resources to reduce costs.

   B. Configure compute resources to match the processing needs of the batch job.

   C. Use the same compute configuration as for online services.

   D. Ignore the volume of data being processed.

3. Incorporating MLOps: How should MLOps practices be applied when new data is available?

   A. Ignore new data until the model performance declines significantly.

   B. Manually retrain the model once a year.

   C. Automate model retraining based on new data additions.

   D. Disable event-based triggers to simplify operations.

Thought experiment answers

This section contains the solutions to the thought experiment. Each answer explains why the answer choice is correct.

1. The answer is **B.** Configuring settings for online deployment tailored to the model's requirements ensures that the model performs optimally by adapting to specific computational and operational needs. Options A, C, and D do not address the necessity of customized configurations for peak performance.

2. The answer is **B.** Configuring compute resources to match the processing needs of the batch job is critical to ensure efficient handling of the data and computational demands, particularly for large datasets or complex processing tasks. Options A, C, and D overlook the importance of aligning resources with specific batch job requirements.

3. The answer is **C.** Automating model retraining based on new data additions ensures that the model stays current and accurate, adapting continuously to changes in input data. This practice is essential in MLOps to maintain model efficacy over time. Options A, B, and D do not leverage the benefits of automation and real-time data integration in maintaining model performance.

## CHAPTER 5

Exam DP-100: Designing and Implementing a Data Science Solution on Azure—updates

The purpose of this chapter

For Chapters 1–4, the content should remain relevant throughout the life of this edition. But for this chapter, we will update the content over time. Even after you purchase the book, you'll be able to access a PDF file online with the most up-to-date version of this chapter.

Why do we need to update this chapter after the publication of this book? For these reasons:

- To add more technical content to the book before the next edition is published. This updated PDF chapter will include additional technology content.

- To communicate details about the next version of the exam, to tell you about our publishing plans for that version, and to help you understand what that means to you.

- To provide an accurate mapping of the current exam objectives to the existing chapter content. Although exam objectives evolve, and products are renamed, most of the content in this book will remain accurate and relevant. The online chapter will cover the content of any new objectives, as well as provide explanatory notes on how the new objectives map to the current text.

After the initial publication of this book, Microsoft Press will provide supplemental updates as digital downloads for minor exam updates. If an exam has major changes or accumulates enough minor changes, we will then announce a new edition. We will do our best to provide any updates to you free of charge before we release a new edition. However, if the updates are significant enough between editions, we may release the updates as a low-priced stand-alone e-book.

If we do produce a free updated version of this chapter, you can access it on the book's product page. Simply visit *MicrosoftPressStore.com/ERDP100/downloads* to view and download the updated material.

About possible exam updates

Microsoft reviews exam content periodically to ensure that it aligns with the technology and job role associated with the exam. This includes, but is not limited to, incorporating functionality and features related to technology changes, changing skills needed for success within a job role, and revisions to product names. Microsoft updates the exam details page to notify candidates when changes occur. If you have registered this book and an update occurs to this chapter, you will be notified by Microsoft Press about the availability of this updated chapter.

Impact on you and your study plan

Microsoft's information helps you plan, but it also means that the exam might change before you pass the current exam. That impacts you, affecting how we deliver this book to you. This chapter gives us a way to communicate in detail about those changes as they occur. But you should keep an eye on other spaces as well.

For those other information sources to watch, bookmark and check these sites for news:

Microsoft Learn: Check the main source for up-to-date information: *microsoft.com/ learn*. Make sure to sign up for automatic notifications at that page.

Microsoft Press: Find information about products, offers, discounts, and free downloads: *microsoftpressstore.com*. Make sure to register your purchased products.

As changes arise, we will update this chapter with more details about the exam and book content. At that point, we will publish an updated version of this chapter, listing our content plans. That detail will likely include the following:

- Content removed, so if you plan to take the new exam version, you can ignore that content when studying.

- New content planned per new exam topics, so you know what's coming.

The remainder of the chapter shows the new content that may change over time.

News and commentary about the exam objective updates

The current official Microsoft Study Guide for the DP-100 *Designing and Implementing a Data Science Solution on Azure* exam is located at *https://learn.microsoft.com/en-us/credentials/ certifications/resources/study-guides/dp-100*. This page has the most recent version of the exam objective domain.

This statement was last updated in July 2024, before the publication of *Exam Ref DP-100 Designing and Implementing a Data Science Solution on Azure*.

This version of this chapter has no news to share about the next exam release.

Updated technical content

The current version of this chapter has no additional technical content.

Objective mapping

This *Exam Ref* is based on the topics and technologies covered on the exam but is not structured based on the specific order of topics in the exam objectives. Table 5-1 maps the current version of the exam objectives to the chapter content, allowing you to locate where a specific exam objective item is covered without having to consult the index.

TABLE 5-1 Exam objectives mapped to chapters

Exam Objective	Chapter
Design and prepare a machine learning solution	
Design a machine learning solution ■ Determine the appropriate compute specifications for a training workload ■ Describe model deployment requirements ■ Select which development approach to use to build or train a model	1
Manage an Azure Machine Learning workspace ■ Create an Azure Machine Learning workspace ■ Set up Git integration for source control	1
Manage data in an Azure Machine Learning workspace ■ Select Azure storage resources ■ Register and maintain datastores ■ Create and manage data assets	1
Manage compute for experiments in Azure Machine Learning ■ Create compute targets for experiments and training ■ Select an environment for a machine learning use case ■ Configure attached compute resources, including Apache Spark pools ■ Monitor compute utilization	1
Explore data and train models	
Explore data by using data assets and datastores ■ Access and wrangle data during interactive development ■ Wrangle interactive data with Apache Spark	2
Create models by using the Azure Machine Learning Designer ■ Create a training pipeline ■ Consume data assets from Designer ■ Use custom code components in Designer ■ Evaluate the model, including responsible AI guidelines	2

Exam Objective	Chapter
Explore data and train models	
Use automated machine learning to explore optimal models ■ Use automated machine learning for tabular data ■ Select and understand training options, including preprocessing and algorithms ■ Evaluate an automated machine learning run, including responsible AI guidelines ■ Use automated machine learning for computer vision ■ Use automated machine learning for natural language processing (NLP)	2
Use notebooks for custom model training ■ Develop code by using a compute instance ■ Track model training by using MLflow ■ Evaluate a model ■ Train a model by using Python SDKv2 ■ Use the terminal to configure a compute instance	2
Tune hyperparameters with Azure Machine Learning ■ Select a sampling method ■ Define the primary metric ■ Define early termination options	2
Prepare a model for deployment	
Run model training scripts ■ Configure job run settings for a script ■ Configure compute for a job run ■ Consume data from a data asset in a job ■ Run a script as a job by using Azure Machine Learning ■ Use MLflow to log metrics from a job run ■ Use logs to troubleshoot job run errors ■ Configure an environment for a job run ■ Define parameters for a job	3
Implement training pipelines ■ Create a pipeline ■ Pass data between steps in a pipeline ■ Schedule and run a pipeline ■ Monitor pipeline runs ■ Create custom components ■ Use component-based pipelines	3
Manage models in Azure Machine Learning ■ Describe MLflow model output ■ Identify an appropriate framework to package a model ■ Assess a model by using responsible AI guidelines	3

Exam Objective	Chapter
Deploy and retrain a model	
Deploy a model ■ Configure settings for online deployment ■ Configure the compute for a batch deployment ■ Deploy a model to an online endpoint ■ Deploy a model to a batch endpoint ■ Test an online deployed service ■ Invoke the batch endpoint to start a batch scoring job	4
Apply Machine Learning Operations (MLOps) practices ■ Trigger an Azure Machine Learning job, including from Azure DevOps or GitHub ■ Automate model retraining based on new data additions or data changes ■ Define event-based retraining triggers	4

Index

A

account keys, security, 26
ACI (Azure Container Instances), 13
AKS (Azure Kubernetes Service), 125–126
    deploying models as Kubernetes pods, 126
    managing and scaling model deployments, 126
algorithms, 5, 6, 57, 58
AmlCompute cluster, 9
Apache Spark
    data wrangling, 44–47
    execution model, 45
    jobs, 35–36
        resource access, 35–36
        user identity passthrough, 36
    pools, 33, 34–35
Application Insights
    Azure Machine Learning integration, 103–104
    querying and analyzing logs, 107
AUC-ROC, 60
authentication, pipeline, 143
automation
    Azure Machine Learning
        with GitHub, 144–147
        using Azure DevOps, 143–144
    model retraining, 147–148
AutoML, 6, 57
    algorithms, 6, 58
    evaluation metrics, 61–62
    exploring optimal models, 54
    limitations of model complexity, 6–7
    max trials, 59
    model evaluation, 73–74
    for NLP, 67
        configuring the AutoML experiment, 68–69
        selecting the NLP task, 67–68
        setting up the environment, 67
    predicting customer churn, 62–63
    selecting algorithms, 57

selecting training options, 57–58
setting up compute for training, 65–66
submitting a job, 66
using for computer vision, 64
    evaluating and deploying the model, 65–66
    preparing the data, 65
    selecting the task type, 64–65
    setting up the environment, 64
working with tabular data, 55–57
autoscaling, 8–9, 123
    cost management, 9–10
    training clusters, 8–9
az ml batch-deployment command, 137
az ml batch-endpoint create command, 134
az ml batch-endpoint delete command, 137
az ml compute create command, 133
az ml environment create command, 135
az ml job create command, 99
az ml online-endpoint delete command, 132–133
Azure CLI, 20
    commands
        az ml batch-deployment, 137
        az ml batch-endpoint create, 134
        az ml batch-endpoint delete, 137
        az ml compute create, 133
        az ml environment create, 135
        az ml job create, 99
        az ml online-endpoint delete, 132–133
        execution context, 86
        input format, 85
        kubectl, 126
        ssh, 92
    deleting online endpoints, 132–133
    interacting with the workspace, 19
    running a pipeline, 99–100
Azure Container Registry, 13

B

C

centralized logging, 104
classification metrics, 60, 73
cloud environment, logging, 105
cluster
    AKS (Azure Kubernetes Service), 125–126
    compute, 8–9, 84
code
    compute target, 30
    configuring training options, 59–60
    converting CSV file to MLTable, 56–57
    creating an interactive PCP using Plotly, 155–156
    custom, 49–51
    defining script parameters, 94
    implementing preprocessing steps needed to train a model, 43–44
    running your AutoML experiment, 63–64
    ScriptRunConfig, 93–94
    selecting compute targets for an experiment, 31
    selecting the best model from an AutoML run, 61–62
    Spark pool for reading large datasets and preprocessing tasks, 45–47
    submitting a AutoML NLP job, 68
    working with tabular data, 100
    YAML pipeline, 97
command/s
    az ml batch-deployment, 137
    az ml batch-endpoint create, 134
    az ml batch-endpoint delete, 137
    az ml compute create, 133
    az ml environment create, 135
    az ml job create, 99
    az ml online-endpoint delete, 132–133
    execution context, 86
    input format, 85
    kubectl, 126
    ssh, 92
complexity, model, 5–7
components, YAML pipeline, 98–99
compute
    Apache Spark pool, 33
    autoscaling, 8–9
    clusters, 8–9, 84
    configuring for a job run, 84
    managed, 4–5
    resources, attaching to Jupyter notebook, 70–71
    serverless, 5, 34
    setting up for training, 65–66

targets, 4, 8
    Azure Machine Learning, 2–3
    creating, 26–28
    idempotence, 30
    selecting for an experiment, 30–31
    selecting VM size, 7–8
    unmanaged, 5
    utilization, metrics, 36–37
Conda YAML file, 135
confusion matrix, 61
connecting to the workspace, 19
containerization, 126
context-aware MLOps, 154
CPU-based instance types, 123–124
creating
    batch deployment, 134–135
    batch endpoint, 133–134
    compute targets, 26–28
    custom components, 107–108
    datasets, 27–28
    datastore, 26, 43
    environment, 32
    training pipeline, 48, 95–99
    workspace, 15
cron, 102
CSV file, converting to MLTable, 56–57
curated environment, 32–33
custom code, 49–51
custom components, 109–110
    creating, 107–108
    registration, 108
custom dimensions, 106–107
customer churn, predicting, 62–63

D

DAG (directed acyclic graph), 50
data
    accessing, 42
    cleaning and preparation, 151
    collection/ingestion, 150
    exploration, 41, 42, 43
    featurization, 59
    preprocessing, 49
    tabular, 55–57, 100
    wrangling, 42, 44–47
data lake storage, 24
data science, 1

pass data between steps, 100–101
running with Azure CLI, 99–100
scheduling, 101–103
steps and components, 98–99
policy/ies, 5
data retention and deletion, 10
early termination, 78
job autotermination, 10
precision-recall curve, 61
predicting, customer churn, 62–63
preprocessing data for model training, 49
primary metric, 59, 60, 78
privacy, Responsible AI Standard, 53–54
production deployment strategies, 124–125
Python, 42
script, 49–50, 105
SDK 2.0
installing and interacting with, 17–18
training a model, 74–75

Q-R

querying logs in Application Insights, 107
quota change, 7

random sampling, 76–77
random_split() method, 100
recommender system, 54
registration, custom component, 108
regression metrics, 61
remote VM, 4
Reserved Instances, 10
residuals plot, 61
Responsible AI Standard, 51–52, 111
explainability, 53
fairness, 52–53
model assessment, 114–115
privacy and security, 53–54
retraining, 152
automation, 147–148
triggers, 148–150
RMSE (root mean squared error), 61
ROC curve, 61
rolling updates, 124
R-squared, 61
run() function, 138
run record, 16
run.get_details() method, 28

S

safe rollout strategy, 124
sampling
Bayesian, 77–78
grid, 77
random, 76–77
scaling, auto, 8–9
schedule, pipeline, 101–103
scoring script, testing, 138–139
ScriptRunConfig, 93–94
script/s. See also job/s
parameters, 94
Python, 49–50, 105
scoring, 138–139
training, 81–82
accessing data, 84
integrating MLFlow, 86–87
running as a job, 84–86
settings, 82–83
SDK, Azure Machine Learning, 17–18
secrets, 144
security
account keys, 26
authentication, 143
model deployment, 13
Responsible AI Standard, 53–54
sentiment analysis, 44–45
serverless compute, 5, 34
SLA (service-level agreement), monitoring, 131–132
Sobol sampling, 77
Spark pool, 34–35
Spark Pools, 4
SSH, for debugging, 91–93
ssh command, 92
storage, 23–25
datastore
creating, 26
register and maintain, 25–26
structured logging, 106

T

tabular data, 55–57
take_sample() method, 100
terminal
accessing, 75–76
streaming logs to, 90

testing
   batch endpoint, 139
   online deployment, 137–138
   scoring script, 138–139
traces, 88, 107
tracking data in experiments, 28
training, 41, 57, 151
   in batch, 12
   clusters, 8–9
   cost management, 10
   development approach, 14
   distributed, 58
   jobs. *See* job/s
   parallelized, 10
   pipeline, 94–95
      creating, 48, 95–99
      custom components, 107–108, 109–110
      logging, 104–107
      modules, 50–51
      monitoring, 103
      pass data between steps, 100–101
      running with Azure CLI, 99–100
      schedule, 101–103
      steps and components, 98–99
   preparing data in Jupyter notebook, 71
   preprocessing steps, 43–44
   re-, 147–148, 152
   script, 81–82
      integrating MLFlow, 86–87
      job run, 84–86
      settings, 82–83
   tracking models, 72–73
   using Python SDKv2, 74–75
   validation strategy, 59
   workload. *See also* workload
      autoscaling, 8–9
      compute specifications, 2–3
      model complexity, 5–7
      selecting VM size, 7–8
transparency, 53
triggers, event-based retraining, 148–150
troubleshooting
   common errors, 140
   job run errors, 88–90
tuning hyperparameters, 76
   Bayesian sampling, 77–78
   define the primary metric, 78
   grid sampling, 77
   random sampling, 76–77

U-V

unmanaged compute, 5
URIs, Azure storage service, 25

version control, 22
viewing, utilization metrics, 36–37
Visual Studio Code, 21
visualizations, 61–62, 155–156
visualizing Pareto tradeoffs, 154–156
VM (virtual machine)
   GPU optimized, 8
   Low-Priority, 10
   remote, 4
   size, 7, 8
   types, 7–8

W

workload
   autoscaling, 8–9
      cost management, 9–10
      training clusters, 8–9
   compute specifications, 2–3
   model complexity, 5–7
   selecting VM size, 7–8
workspace, 15
   accessing the terminal, 75–76
   connecting to, 19
   creating, 15
   interacting with, 18, 19
   organizing, 16–17
   run record, 16
   storage resources, 23–25
   tasks performed in, 16

X-Y-Z

YAML
   configuration file, 135
   pipeline file, 96–99